I am grateful for all the support Mark Green has provided to me and so many others in the R&B and Hip-Hop community. Mark Green's hard work has significantly impacted our careers, helping us achieve our dreams and reach new heights. Mark's belief in my talent was proven by unwavering support. God Bless Mark Green. Thank you for everything.

—*Dr. Rev. Kurtis Blow Walker, Hip-Hop Artist*

In an industry that gets a bad rap on integrity and honesty, Mark shines through as a man of trust and hard work. Maybe because he's old school, but he's a good person as a representative of our culture and our industry.

—*Chubb Rock, Hip-Hop Artist*

Mark Green is a remarkable individual with a gentle demeanor and a heart of gold. Mark's unwavering dedication and determination have been instrumental in championing my aspirations across the globe. He is undoubtedly poised to secure the bag effortlessly. Beyond being my exceptional agent, Mark has become a cherished friend. As a female Hip-Hop pioneer, his ability to collaborate with me and uphold the true essence of my mission and talent is commendable. We deeply appreciate his relentless efforts and applaud his ongoing success in not only supporting me, but also making significant strides in his field. Once again, Mark has achieved another groundbreaking milestone.

—*Yo-Yo, Hip-Hop Artist*

I always tell everyone that Mark Green was the manager who taught me the difference between being an artist and a star. The one person in the industry who wasn't out to rob me. He was sometimes like a manager, sometimes like a father, but always like a brother. These are stories that need to be told!

—*Rome JD Boogie Boys, Hip-Hop Artist*

I first became familiar with Mark when I interviewed Master Gee of The Sugarhill Gang. Gee mentioned an upperclassman who put him on to rap music, and I dug a little deeper. Mark has a wealth of knowledge concerning the early days of my favorite record label, and I'm honored to call him a friend.

—*Historian Jay Quan*

In an industry designed to make sure you have a very short life span, multiplied by X 10 X when it comes to Hip-Hop, Mark has found work for me personally, where there is seemingly no work available. He's one of my favorite people, period.

—*Kool Mo Dee, Hip-Hop Artist*

What an experience working with Mark. He has always been about his business, his word is his bond, a straight shooter and a good brother, and believe me, that is a rarity in the entertainment industry.

—*Hendogg of the Sugar Hill Gang, Hip-Hop Artist*

Mark Green is known for booking solid shows and his professionalism has made him one of the top agents in the game. Mark and Celebrity Talent Agency have been part of my Hip-Hop journey for many years and I am proud to be on his roster.

—*Rob Base, Hip-Hop Artist*

I have known Mark for many decades and can assure you that music, entertainment, and business acumen have been in his blood since day one. While the rest of us have corpuscles, Mark has the entertainment business surging through his veins. Mark is second to none in his industry and will literally go to the ends of the earth to ensure that the bottom line is met. He is a man amongst men, a force to be reckoned with, a man for all seasons. An industry legend, these pages only describe his exoskeleton as they can never define the mind within. Hang on and enjoy the ride…these stories are priceless.

—*Todd Hardy, classmate & friend*

Mark is a consummate music industry executive who always does his absolute best for his clients and the people with whom he works. Having him on my team to build The Hip-Hop Museum has been an absolute pleasure.

—*Rocky Bucano, Executive Director of the Hip-Hop Museum*

"There should be a picture of Mark under the term "team player." He has been on my team at three different music companies. I wouldn't have had it any other way!

—*Glynice Coleman, VP EMI Records and VP Humility Records*

Mark Green is someone I've known for decades in the entertainment industry. He was my booking agent in 1986 when my record was out. He is humble and gracious, a brother willing to work with you, and a brother I've always been fond of. He's remained cool, calm, and collected. He has worked with many celebrities and artists over the years, no matter how young or old.

—*Vansilk, Hip-Hop Producer*

Mark Green has taken his amazing talents from promoting records to owning one of the most prestigious booking agencies in the entertainment industry! He is a great guy with great relationships. I am excited for all to read his book, learn from his journey and lock into some real "gems." Congratulations to my buddy!

—*Bo Sampson, MCA Records*

Mark and I were both enamored by everything about music. His journey is the result of that. Mark did the work to support his dream, and I'm proud of him for that and so much more.

—*Freddie Williams, classmate & friend*

# *The* Show Must Go On

## Backstage Stories of a Hip-Hop Agent

## MARK "MONEY" GREEN

### WITH ERICKA WILLIAMS

Published by Mynd Matters Publishing
www.myndmatterspublishing.com

978-1-963874-08-2 (pbk)
978-1-963874-09-9 (hdc)
978-1-963874-10-5 (ebk)

Photo credits: Fred Williams / Perren Media Group (page 26 & 27), Dean Boyer (page 64), Kevin Rose (page 31)

FIRST EDITION

*In memory of my father, Elbert L. Green, my mother, Ethel J. Green, and my daughter, Janay I. Green.*

*You were my guiding light, uplifting me through my life's darkest and most promising days. You have stood by me through the test of time. You are forever in my heart, spirit, and mind. Love you forever. Rest in peace.*

# FOREWORD

I am Guy O'Brian, but professionally known to the world as Master Gee. I want to say a few things about Mark Green, so you know, and in my estimation, Mark Green is the kind of guy that is a doer; he's the kind of guy that makes things happen. I've known him since high school, and he is literally the first person that I ever heard rap, so one, he's the reason I am who I am today because without me hearing Mark, I would have never known rapping was even being done. Therefore, I would have never written a rap or recorded a rap. There would be no Master Gee if there were no Mark Green second; the thing is, not only did he always show entrepreneurial abilities, but he was always the trendsetter. He's always been the kind of person that, in the background, made it the front ground. What I mean by that is this entertainment business is a business, and unless you have people like Mark Green around to take care of the business, then it makes no sense. So, you know, he's the kind of guy that many people need to recognize that if it weren't for Mark Green, their careers wouldn't be what they've ended up being. He's managed, he's been an executive, he's been in the Ins and outs, he's managed venues. He's the kind of person that, in my estimation, is a mover and a shaker. So, this book and anything that he ever does, I'm 100% on board with, and it couldn't be done or concerning a better person than Mark Green.

*Master Gee, Sugarhill Gang*

# The Show Must Go On

# CONTENTS

CHAPTER 1

# IT WAS ALL A DREAM

**M**usic is my life. Those were the words written in my high school yearbook. From the time I can remember, I never thought about anything else. There was something about music that just drove my instincts. Night after night I would stay up until the wee hours watching Elvis movies and Soul Train. I would study the dance moves, recite the lyrics, and know every musician who played on every record. All I wanted was to learn how to play every instrument and become a star! During the day, I would go down to our basement and crank up the old stereo console and begin to play my mother's records: The Drifters, Dionne Warrick, The Platters, you name it. Whatever she had, I listened.

Once I got a paper route and was able to buy my own records, that's all I did. I saved every penny until Saturday. That's when I would walk down to Main Street and into the record shop. As soon as I stepped inside, I was in heaven. I would buy two to three records every week, learn all the words, and read up on all the musicians. I would walk anywhere that there was a record store because each store brought a new light and a new history lesson. That's because the guy who would sell you the record was like a music guru. He would talk about the beat and describe the baseline and would fill your mind with delightful sounds that would be circulated over and over and over in your head.

By 1969, there was a new group that debuted their first single, and they were all around the same age as me. Man, I could not believe it. The song was "I Want You Back," and they were known as The Jackson 5. I ran to the music store to purchase the record and began to learn every word. The next day, I asked my mother if I could take some music lessons, and the first thing she did was sign me up to learn a crazy-looking machine called the accordion. *What in the world is this*, I asked myself. It had keys like a typewriter on one end and knobs like a TV on the other end. Then you had to squeeze it together like a sponge. It was heavy and awkward, and after about three lessons, I told her I didn't want to learn that instrument.

I was sad and depressed because I wanted to play a *real* instrument like the drums or the guitar. Before I could even express my concern, she set me up to take clarinet lessons. As soon as the guy appeared at my house with that instrument, the first thing I thought was, *This is a girl's instrument! Why would she do this to me?* However, after about six months, I started getting good at it. My teacher was happy, my mom was ecstatic, but I hated it. As the year came to an end, I was playing clarinet in the school band. But in my mind, I wanted to play drums and nothing else. It wasn't until the following year that my life changed along with my dreams.

It was 1970. I was eleven, and they told me I'd never walk again. Who would have thought that later I would become a black belt in martial arts, a track star, a musician, and an Omega Psi Phi Step Champion? I did all those things and then some.

My passion for music drowned out the screams from my mom for me to "Turn that damn music down!" as I grooved to the sounds of George Clinton, The Meters, James Brown, and The Drifters. My mother loved music and she had a lot of records in her collection. She loved to sing and played piano by ear. I think she enjoyed the fact that I had a love for music as well. We never really talked about my love for music because they were more concerned about me doing my schoolwork and preparing for college.

One day while home sick with a cold, I laid on the couch watching *I Love Lucy*. When I got up to turn the channel, I lost my balance and fell flat on my face. An excruciating pain radiated throughout my left leg, so I just laid there crying. It was like that numb  feeling you get in your leg or foot when you've sat too long and it's fallen asleep. When my parents came home, I told them I could not move my left leg. My father picked me up and put me in the car and rushed me to the hospital. After they checked me out, they put me in a room that was secluded and quarantined like I had the plague. Finding out that I not only had pneumonia but would probably never walk again was the scariest thing I'd ever faced.

For three months, I stayed in a hospital bed and watched out of the window as winter turned to spring. My spirit diminished. I remember being moved out of the "contagious" room, which was blocked off with yellow tape and anyone entering had to wear a hazmat suit to enter, to a "real" room. My roommate was related to a famous football player for the NY Giants named Richie Kotite, whose presence and stardom made me hungry to succeed and defy the odds that were stacked against me.

For some reason, day after day, I was in constant pain, not knowing why. It was as though it would never go away. I felt so alone, and the aching did not help. Only one of my classmates came to see me, and that was to bring my classwork. I thought about school, but more than that, I wanted to walk again. I know the nurses got tired of me ringing that buzzer, but that's all I could do. I looked forward to seeing them daily because I had no other connection to family. My parents were at work, my sister Lori was too young to know what was going on, and I didn't have any visitors. The nurses would spend time reading and talking to me and encouraging me by saying things would get better. Every day, there was always a doctor or a nurse coming to administer some type of medicine.

The agony of having nurses threaten me that long needles would get stuck in my back if I moved during a spinal tap to doctors repeating that I would never walk all dissipated the day the doctor checked to see if I could feel my legs. The doctor hit me with a percussion hammer, and I could not feel it. What I did feel every night was the excruciating pain of what I can only imagine as my legs being cut with knives. Even the sheets hurt my legs. It felt like I was laying on a bed of broken glass and every time I moved, I was being sliced or cut to the point that special lambskin sheets had to be ordered to minimize the torment. I had seven specialists from other states and countries, including India and Germany, and no one could figure out what or why I could not walk. After a while, I got used to being in a wheelchair and life seemed to be what it was going to be. However, every now and then, I would go back to wanting to be healed.

Another ray of sunshine through that cloudy period of my life was my parents visiting me every day after they would get off of work and eventually making my own fun by racing my wheelchair down the hospital hallways. But the agony returned upon hearing the shriek of my mother's anguish when she learned I wouldn't walk again. As she would for the rest of her life, she regained composure through her faith and passed it down to me when she said that I should just "keep praying and asking God for healing." At the time, I didn't see it as tangible advice. But over time, I grew to believe more and more that God would be there for me as He proved himself to be many times after that.

My mother was a woman of faith who spent her whole life being devoted to the Lord. She began to teach me about God from the day I could read. The Bible stories and Black history lessons are what we studied weekly. It was imperative that I went to Sunday School and then spend the rest of the day in church. As time would allow, she later became the head of the church plays and eventually became the superintendent of the Sunday School. As I grew old enough to make my own decisions, I was always reminded that If I could stay out and party to the wee hours on a Friday or Saturday night, I could get up and go to church on Sunday morning too. That was the rule in our house. No matter what time you came in, you better be up for breakfast with your suit on and ready for church.

Part of my therapy that brought some comfort was the water treatment. Every day, we had what I called my water sport, where I would get in the pool and try to swim using my upper body with my legs in tow. As a young kid, I always enjoyed swimming. So being in the pool was enjoyable and gave me a feeling of hope. After my lessons, I would get out of the pool, and they would exercise my legs with their hands by moving my legs up and down. However, my prayers to God and my trust are what I believe was the remedy that would eventually give me back feeling in my legs and a new start in life.

After exercising, stretching, and tending to my legs inside and outside of the pool, the day finally came when my leg was hit yet again with the reflex hammer, but this time, I could feel it! I could not believe it. I screamed and yelled, "I feel it! I feel it!" I cried and thanked God repeatedly. God was truly a good God, and I was ecstatic!

Unfortunately, the next challenge came when the doctors realized that the inactivity of my legs had caused my muscles to constrict and shrink. One leg had become shorter than the other. If you're thinking, "No way," that is exactly what I said at the time. I had to wear a special shoe that looked more like a wedge heel that a woman would wear. Talk about embarrassing and spirit-crushing again. The correct term for it is a custom orthotic. For me, it was an ugly ass scene with me walking with a crawler and deformed footwear. I could only walk two steps, and then I would have to pick the contraption up and propel it ahead of me to take two small steps to catch up with it. Imagine a teen boy with an old man walker. This was my daily routine for weeks. Every day, I would walk up and down the block, determined to walk again. Whatever it took, I was ready. I continued until, eventually, my muscle stretched and caught back up to its counterpart, and I went from "walker gang" to "cane gang." It was refreshing, but now I walked with a limp.

I acquired a love for working out. I would spend hours in the gym, working mostly on my legs. I could feel the muscles developing. I spent day after day walking up and down the block, running up hills, stadium stairs, and city blocks. I decided to sign up for the track team so I could get in shape for football. I loved the sport and could not wait until the day I would be a starting varsity player. I would spend time doing the two-mile run, hating every minute and then finishing with sprints. My coach continued to work with me and encouraged me daily. He saw something I didn't. Eventually, I made the track team and began to run sprints and set goals and break records. I even ran in the Penn Relays and West Point track meets, to name a few.

One night while working out before a meet the following day, a friend convinced me to smoke a joint telling me I would run faster. I was psyched because I had a big matchup at West Point. The coach only took two of us, me and another sprinter. I was already making a name for myself and had big hopes of winning that track meet. I came in last place and my coach was furious. I was so out of breath it felt like my chest was about to explode.

"What happened out there? You look like you had rigor mortis." The coach looked at me after asking.

I told him I didn't know, it just didn't feel right. I vowed to myself that I would never do drugs again. As I got my groove back, I became the anchor on all the relay teams, set school records, and got my varsity letter in track. I loved running relays and the competition that came with being the anchor. What was birthed out of tragedy turned me into a track star who accumulated many trophies and accolades. All praises to God!

Simultaneously, my passion for music was reignited as I began taking piano and drum lessons and going to the library and researching the different careers in the music industry. I still have the book that I *borrowed* from the library in eighth grade which was my bible of how I was going to become a celebrity.

## CHAPTER 2

# BLACK PEARL

Freddie William was a neighbor who became my friend and brother in music. We were both in the eighth-grade chorus and shared a love for music. He played the guitar and after many conversations, we decided to form a band and call it "Black Pearl." The first day I went to his home, I was in shock by the gold and platinum albums on his living room wall of The Jackson Five because his uncle, Freddie Perren, wrote and produced for them. I could not believe what I was seeing. I was in a daze and just stared at the wall. *This is it! This is what I want!* At that moment, I had made a best friend, and I wholeheartedly believed that "Black Pearl" would soon have plaques of

*Freddie Williams*

their own and give The Jackson 5 a run for their money.

Black Pearl had made a name in the community and would perform at cocktail sips, house parties, and anywhere my dad and another of our band member's parents, Saul Brevard Sr., could book us. We would spend days practicing in my basement and focusing on the prize of

becoming famous like The Jackson 5. My father thought so, too, and decided to be our manager and direct our path. We were working every weekend and making money. Our group consisted of Tim Ellison on piano, Stanley Alston on lead guitar, Freddie Williams on guitar, Saul Brevard and Mike Hardy on trumpet, Glenn Toby on bass, Sandy Williams on trombone, Dawn Rogers and Nancy Brevard on lead vocals, and me on the drums. We had uniforms that consisted of

*Black Pearl Band*

black pants, white turtlenecks, and big 70s "pimp hats" that were black velvet with a white band and a long feather on the side. We looked like a professional band. We played all the 70s hits and became a local cover band in the neighborhood. Some of my favorite songs that we played were "Skin Tight" by the Ohio Players, "Dream Merchant" by New Birth, and "Supernature" by Ben E. King.

Eventually, we recorded a record in a real studio that was owned by a local R&B artist named Too Sweet. The studio had two rooms to record and perform. I remember walking in and seeing egg cartons all over the wall. I had never been in a studio but was still taken back by the egg cartons. Too Sweet looked more like Steve Urkel than a music star, but he had a following because he did a lot of shows in the hood. He'd made a couple of records and became "ghetto famous." So, we looked at

him as someone who almost made it.

As we continued playing wherever we could, I continued to excel in sports. One summer, as I played in a summer league basketball game, I got into a fight with a preacher's son. We knew each other from church, and we all played ball in the same hood, but we weren't close. Fighting for me was never a problem, I actually enjoyed it and had been suspended from school several times for it. However, the fact that I was getting the best of him—or should I say proceeding to beat his ass, he pulled out a knife and stabbed me on the side of my back. As he went for my face, I threw up my hand and he slashed it, causing temporary paralysis in my hand. The blood ran down my fingers and arm like water from a faucet. The cut was so deep I could see the bones in my hand. Three of my fingers had lost sensation and I didn't regain feeling in them until I entered college two years later.

It put a damper on my piano playing and to top it off, I ended up playing on the same football team as that dude. It bothered me that I had to share the field with him. The first month, I had to practice with a cast on my hand. I was not able to do much on offense but on defense, I tried to do my best to dislocate something on his body. Just before the season

*Mark Green*

started, I had the cast removed but still had problems with sensation in three of my fingers.

I loved football and had been playing since I was in elementary school. I started every year from junior varsity all the way up to my senior year. A friend nicknamed me "LC Greenwood" after a football player from the Pittsburg Steelers, and that name followed me through high school. I really had a bright future in football, but during one important game, I dropped the ball on a pass due to the lack of feeling in my hand, and my future career as a tight end went down the drain. I did not want to tell my coach that I was handicapped and unable to feel three fingers. Although I was the kicker and the punter as well, my coach didn't care. He benched me. I was angry with him and the ongoing situation with my hand. The following week, I became the backup player. I was insulted and angry, so I quit the sport I loved and lived to regret it.

Every time I look back in my yearbook or meet teammates who talk about football, I sulk. By our third game, I had received letters from some small colleges to play football and I threw it all away. However, I learned a big lesson that stuck with me through the rest of my life: NEVER QUIT! To this day, I live by the reminder to always see things through. I'd rather suffer and hurt before I give in.

That left my other passion alive and well. At the urging of my music teacher, who persuaded me to believe that I had to choose music or sports, I delved into the former and made a whole life of it. My teacher had already expressed that I needed to make a choice. I was bulking up for football however, all that weightlifting was making me stiff behind the drums. So, when I left football, the decision was made…I was going to stick to music.

* * *

It had been more than two years and Freddie Williams and I decided to contact his uncle, The Jackson 5 producer Freddie Perren, to see if we were on the road to riches with our songs. Time revealed that we were nowhere in their league, let alone anywhere close to being famous.

*Mark Green (LC) & David Heard (Rock Bottom)*

By this time, the disco era had begun and was not only changing America but dissolving the funk era. Yes, this new sound was taking over and impacting the world. Djs were becoming more of the stars than the actual groups. There was a new dance out called the Hustle, and other dance moves started forming, like the Bump, Boogaloo, and the Robot. Even the fashion had changed. Black Pearl was on its last leg and had to say its goodbyes. But give up music? Not I. There were two other DJs in the hood that I knew. One was AJ

Savage and the other was an upcoming group called Sound On Sound. At that point, I had all the equipment in my basement including the giant Peavey speakers we used for our band, four ten-inch speakers in each cabinet that could rock any party. My DJ life was birthed. I turned up the volume on the speakers and began "borrowing" my mom's records and training myself on how to rock a party. I would spend days and nights practicing. Times were different back then because the mixers we used didn't have a crossfader where you could hear the beats of two turntables simultaneously. You had to keep one earphone on your ear to hear what was playing on one turntable and then listen to the music that was playing through the speakers with your other ear. Then you had to try and time the music to both records to match the beat. That technique came easy to me, and I mastered it in no time.

My first gig as "DJ LC" was at a party at Hackensack High School and a legend was born. I was named "LC" on the football field and decided to keep it for the 1s and 2s. How could I lose? I opened my set with Parliament's "Flashlight," "Play that Funky Music White Boy," Peter Brown, and more. That one event opened up so many other opportunities. I was booked and busy and bringing in duckets, darlings, and lots of dap (translation = money, women, and respect).

I expanded into doing parties in Paterson, Newark, and many project recreation centers, and I gained a large following. I brought on my homie, David Heard, aka "Rock Bottom," to assist me in rocking the parties. Unbeknownst to me, not only were local kids enamored with me, but I had caught the eye of some up-and-coming artists who were about to blow up.

One Saturday night in Englewood, New Jersey, while performing at an Englewood Rec Center, I was approached by a promoter who asked me to be part of a DJ battle in New York. The year was 1977 and I was ecstatic because although I was known in Jersey, I wanted to get around the other popular DJs across the George Washington Bridge in what is now known as the birthplace of Hip-Hop, The "Boogie Down Bronx." I was familiar with the Bronx and Harlem because they were the closest areas to where I lived. Harlem was four miles away, and the Bronx was nine miles. As teenagers, we spent most of our time in Manhattan and Harlem. However, the Bronx was always an option. We often found our way to Club 371 in the Bronx with our fake IDs, which we brought on 42$^{nd}$ Street in the city. I had no problem driving to the Bronx that night by myself.

## CHAPTER 3

# DJ SAVED MY LIFE

The day came and I was on my way to the Bronx. I was alone and there were three other DJ crews that I had to compete against. My crew was me, myself, and I because Rock Bottom couldn't hang on a school night like I could. My parents were supportive of my endeavors and had accepted that I would constantly be "running in the streets" to realize my dreams of stardom and fortune.

I unloaded my car, carried my equipment into the gym, and wired up. No sooner than I could find my records, the promoter told me to crank it up. So, I opened my set with a James Brown track and then moved to "Dance to the Drummer's Beat." There were certain tracks that DJs would play to get the party going. We would always search for the songs that had the break beats and we would extend the song once we saw the b boys take over the dance floor. I had the crowd's attention as I played my set. There were about fifty to seventy-five people standing around dancing to my music. Just as I was "warming up," the other crew started DJing on the other side of the gymnasium. They not only caught the crowd's attention, but most of the spectators had abandoned my stage for those across from me leaving only fifteen people still standing in front of me. There was a big commotion and I wanted to know why my audience had left me high and dry. I quickly ended my set and packed up my equipment and was drawn to the excitement that had taken over. When I got to my competition's "door," I realized that not only were they playing music, they had two performers who were talking to the beat of the music and saying words that rhymed in an intriguing melodic delivery. They had us all in a trance as we watched them dance and talk a talk that was new to my ears.

As they were in the height of their set, another crew began to do what I saw this crew do. And I must say it was apparent that they were rocking the mic in a way that made their crowd want to stay. With so much excitement and allure, I couldn't wait to get home and adopt this new technique, because I knew I could DJ and I knew I could speak. At the time, we didn't have a real name for the sound, we just called it rap because growing up, the term rapping was associated with delivering some slick words when speaking to a woman that you wanted to impress. If you were corny and didn't know how to win her over, she would say, "He ain't got no rap." So, it was important to deliver some slick lines.

The year was 1977. But in the Bronx, this underground sound had been going on since 1973. During this time, the NY radio DJs would take a small line and rhyme them together when they were delivering the new sounds. My two favorite jocks were Hank Spann and Frankie Crocker. The station in NY was WWRL, an AM station. Although FM stations were around, all the Black music that we listened to were on WWRL. It was 1972 when WBLS turned on the radio to FM and Frankie Crocker hit the airwaves with the saying, "If Frankie Crocker isn't on your radio, then your radio isn't really on." Frankie would open his set with his rhyme and wisdom.

*"More dips in your hip, more cut in your strut, and more glide in your stride."*
*"Any time you want me, I'm your guy."*
*"You can hear the Frankie Crocker sound when the sun goes down."*

As early as 1970, DJs would get on the radio and drop their rhymes with music in the background. However, the disco era had already started during the early 70s and began to take over the airwaves and only continued to grow bigger throughout.

I was hyped to perform my song for the first time. The chance came at the Hackensack Projects Rec Center. The crowd went wild as I delivered a sound that would soon be a new genre of music. I was the man, and all the girls and guys would request me to do a live rendition of that track whenever I came around. When school was in session the following Monday, I performed it for all who asked for it, and I loved it. By that time, my DJ bookings had me busy and I was a "hood star."

Out of nowhere I was approached by Gerry Bledsoe, a national DJ from WWRL. He hired me to be a guest DJ on his new show, "Soul Alive," which aired on WPIX channel 11. Gerry was one of the top DJs on WWRL. He had a cool vibe and lived around Teaneck, New Jersey. The show was based on high schools and in the vein of American Bandstand or Soul Train. They would go to different high schools and have the students do the latest dances and create the same type of vibe as the other shows. At the time I was confident because I had been getting requests to DJ at parties and I had a knack for hits.

October 15, 1977 was a day I will never forget. It was my first chance at stardom and my first flop. The event was a chance of a lifetime. But by the end of it, I needed a lifeline. My television debut was short of amazing because they wanted me to wear a stupid top hat that had Guest DJ in bold on the front of it. I felt not only like a clown but like a cornball. It just wasn't my style. Their insistence on me wearing the hat took my focus and my flow. It destroyed my excitement, and the show did not go how I imagined it would.

In between sets of me DJing, I had a dance partner, Delores, who I would dance with on the show. We would do the hustle to the latest songs. I remember us dancing to "NY City Girl." Delores would keep me calm and encourage me to continue despite that stupid hat. We spent the whole day taping. There was an audition to get on the show and you had to be picked by the casting agent. After the audition, I found out Delores made it, and I asked her to be my dance partner.

That's how Delores and I came together.

Nevertheless, that snafu did not diminish my ascension into Ghetto Super Stardom. I still had the popularity and the accolades as the one who brought a new sound to my part of town. By then, I was interning at a radio station at Fairleigh Dickinson University in the neighboring town of Teaneck and spinning the Black and urban music. I had made up my mind that I would be a well-known DJ comparable to Hank Span, whose word play on the airwaves was catchy and slick.

*"Hi this is Hank Spann and I'm more groovier*
*than a five-cent movie where you get your popcorn and*
*candy free."*
*"This is funkier than a cripple crab without a crutch."*

He was the man, and I was becoming the man too. While this new-found fame was building my name, a high school friend of mine, Guy O'Brien, had started following me around and inquiring about the rapping and Djing. He later became known as the rapper, Master Gee. He was part of

*Master Gee*

the Sugarhill Gang, the first rap group to have a song, "Rapper's Delight," played on the radio. Guy and I attended high school together. I was in the 11th grade when he started as a freshman, and we had become friends long before my stardom began. Even with his future fame, he gave credit to me as being the one who introduced him to rap music.

Fast forward to the summer of '78. I was offered a full scholarship in Spanish. However, I had to go to Mexico for the summer and stay with a family to receive it. That was not part of my plan. I was already making a name for myself as a DJ and that is what I wanted to do. At the time I could not image going to a foreign country and staying with someone who did not speak English. I decided to continue working and DJing.

By midsummer, my buddy's uncle Freddie Perren arrived in the area to attend his mother's funeral. Freddie's mother had been murdered by a local guy from Englewood. Although the timing was bad, I was excited when I

*Mark Green & Master Gee*

met Freddie to tell him of my goals of becoming a famous DJ. I had spoken to him several times on the phone, and I lived and breathed every word he said. During that conversation, Freddie told me, "Mark, you don't want to play the music. You want to *make* the music." He also suggested that I go to Howard University and major in Music Education. At the funeral I met the producers of Tavares, LTD, and Black Bird, the Mizell brothers, Larry and Fonce. The group wrote "Boogie Oogie Oogie" by A Taste of Honey and "ABC" and "I Want You Back" by The Jackson 5.

Howard University was smack dab in the middle of the streets of Washington, D.C. and those streets not only looked mean, but Howard lived up to its-reputation as the Harvard of the HBCUs. I had made it thus far without getting caught up in the allure or trap of the hood, but being in college on my own, and free to roam, I saw in my future nothing but trouble if I attended Howard. I was in the streets all through high school and I'd adopted some real bad habits. So, I opted out of that choice and went to Virginia State University. I majored in music and kept my head on straight.

By the time I arrived at college in August of 1978, rap had spread like wildfire. Everybody was getting into the DJ phase, and it seemed like everyone from New York was rapping. It was still new around the other states, but the New York tri-state was in full blast.

I quickly got acclimated to Virginia and made an instant name for myself down there by DJing at two different clubs. One was Mister J's in Petersburg. Mr J's was about two miles from the U.S. Army base and had a stream of traffic yearlong from the recruits. The other club in Richmond was downtown and became the popular club in the area. I was happy with my two DJ gigs working from Thursday through Sunday. Each time I would take students from campus to accompany me to the club. I was making money and a name for myself, but I was also about to get kicked out of college for not attending class. I found myself on probation and my parents were not happy.

By now Master Gee had called and told me that the Sugarhill Gang was making a record off of the song, "Good Times" by Chic. I was astonished, envious, and felt left out. Here I was in college trying to prepare for a career in music and he was not in college but making his dream come true. I considered dropping out. No sooner than he broke his good news and to my despair, the record arrived and I was one of the first DJs to get it. Although excited, I

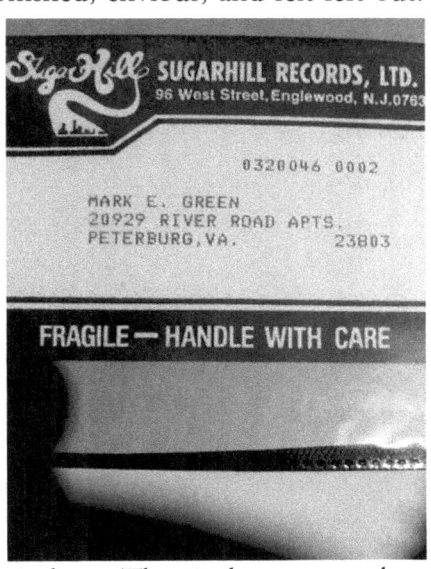

couldn't help feeling a bit jealous. That jealousy turned to pride however, when I was one of the few DJs who had that popular song to spin in the clubs. But "Rapper's Delight" was bittersweet.

Mr. J's had three dance floors and I had started in the smaller first room and then got promoted to the middle room which I kept full all night long. One night I was asked to play the main room and by surprise, it stayed full. As I played "Rapper's Delight," Mr. J came to my booth and told me not to play it anymore because he didn't like it. No sooner than he walked away, I was putting it on my turntable and blasting it through the speakers, because everyone loved that song and had been requesting it all night. I don't even think the first verse was finished by the time I felt someone grabbing and suspending me in the air with his hands around my neck trying to choke the lights out of me. Thank God a few people came to my rescue because when he was done, I not only felt seconds away from my last breath but had the scratches and evidence to prove that the good Lord and some spectators had saved my life.

After we exchanged words, I snatched my picture off the wall, gathered as many records as I could, and made a fast and final exit. I was urged to file a complaint, which I did. The police arrested him, but he was released that same night and able to bully someone else as that was his M.O. I told my parents about my experience and they flew me home later that week to tend to my wounds. When it was time to go, I felt I had no other choice but to steal my father's .38 and .22 pistols to take back with me to Virginia State. I knew I needed more than my gift of gab to protect myself.

# CHAPTER 4

# STREET LIFE

The music business had its ties to the streets and I was not going to let anyone get me. When I returned to Virginia after Thanksgiving break, I found my apartment completely burglarized. The surprise I felt coming into that empty place sent shockwaves to my soul. All my equipment and instruments were gone. Even my clothes, down to my underwear, had been stolen. I had nothing to wear. I stood in complete disbelief right there in the middle of what had been my studio and my solace.

The peace of my bachelor pad started a war in my mind because I was determined to get to the bottom of what had transpired in my spot. Although I had gone to the police to report the crime, I had designated myself the top detective on the case. I knew the only place to find a criminal was in the streets.

Lo and behold, as I was outside in downtown Petersburg, I was totally blindsided by the sight of someone not only wearing my coat, but my pants and my shirt! I recognized the coat as it was bought up north in Macy's, a store that was not retailed down south. I walked up to the guy to have a short conversation. Just to get close enough to open the jacket. Almost instantly, I pulled at my coat and startled the lowlife who was wearing it and we proceeded to have a smash down brawl. We began to fight, and dude bent over and grabbed me by my feet. He unsuccessfully threw me through a store window and escaped to jump on a leaving bus. I almost made it onto the bus except the driver closed the doors not wanting round two to be in his workspace. I made a dash to my car— where my gun was waiting—loaded it and pursued the fleeing bus. I knew the bus would have to stop eventually and I would be there to help him meet his maker.

Fortunately, I was saved from a murder charge when I got stuck at a light and saw a cop sitting at the light to my right. Talk about de-escalation. I thought fast and stashed my pistol and waved the officer down. I was able to report that a perpetrator, who was wearing my clothes, was on the bus and that he should pull it over. I was so relieved when I entered the police station with my wrists free, instead of in cuffs, for taking him out of here. He willfully rode in the patrol car to the station but would soon be read his rights. The cops placed us in separate rooms to get each person's side of the story. As the officer spoke to me, he realized that he had left his notepad with his notes from the other guy's questioning in the room with him and when he returned, the guy had ripped them out as if the officer wouldn't know that he wrote notes from their conversation. (No one has ever accused petty criminals of being geniuses.) So, on that note, homeboy caught a charge. When he was booked, he had foreign money and some jewelry in his pocket that had also been reported missing from my apartment complex.

Weeks later, when we were in court, I just knew I had a win in the bag. Unfortunately, the criminal justice system works for and against us with its technicalities. Long story short, the dude could not be found guilty of robbing my apartment or any other one in the complex because although he was found with the loot, had missed work on the days of the robbery, and his shoe print matched the one that the cops discovered, he was not found on the grounds and there were no witnesses. Technically, he could have purchased the stolen property from the real culprit but in my mind, I pictured him pulling up to my door with a moving van and emptying me out during the Thanksgiving break knowing that no one would be the wiser. During the holidays everyone was likely too busy with their own celebrations and festivities to have noticed or paid this massive operation any mind. It was massive because I lost my DJ equipment, drum set, saxophone, piano, records, clothes, and photos on my wall, which my parents had no intentions of replacing. To give you a better picture, imagine all of my crates of records and then picture them disappearing. Who can DJ without records? It certainly wasn't 2024 and digital DJing had not been birthed yet. My career as a DJ died that weekend. But thankfully, my spirit—although damaged and bruised, was still alive to find the next thing for me to succeed at.

The summer of 1980 approached and I was not going to stop the momentum of getting to the top because by any means necessary was still my M.O. I was determined to get an internship with Sugar Hill Records. I had to be part of the movement that was expeditiously making waves and moving artists up the music charts. My plan to get the job was to go to their studio every day and ask to see the head honcho, Joey Robinson, Sr. He was the man in New Jersey and had the music connection to New York where Hip-Hop was born. He was the king of this new music phenomenon and was making performers national celebrities.

Mr. Robinson was a well-dressed man or as we say in the hood, sugar shit sharp, and very shrewd. He was street savvy and took no shit. He had a gangsta-like persona that put everyone in check. I would go and sit and wait every day trying to meet with him. After the first week of waiting in the lobby, I decided to pack my lunch for the second week because I was not leaving until I met with him, and I guess Mr. Robinson finally realized that because he came out of his office one day, frustrated that he had to at least find out what I wanted.

Mr. Robinson took me upstairs to his office. Papers were scattered around his desk, the phone was ringing, and he seemed to be very impatient. He began our interview by asking me four questions. Can you drive? Do you have a car? Do you know Harlem and the Bronx? Can you work late night and, in the daytime, too? I said yes to everything. He said, "Great you can start tomorrow." I started working as an engineer that same week. If you've ever heard that you should never give up, I am cosigning that advice.

My first assignment was to deliver records and pick up checks in Harlem and the Bronx and all record "one stops" across the George Washington Bridge. A one stop was a big warehouse where they stored records. All the record stores would either go there to purchase records or they would order them to be shipped to their store. I was a "runner" by day and training as an engineer in the studio at night. I would take boxes and boxes of records and deliver them to all the one stops in the area. My whole day was Sugar Hill business, but it was building my future without me even realizing it fully.

The studio was large, but everything seemed to be easily accessible. I learned my way around Mr. Robinson's and the accountant Milton's offices who everyone knew because you had to see him to get your check. I spent all of my time in the studio and on the main floor. There were so many people

*Billy Jones (House Engineer)*

coming in and out of the building. On any given day there'd be a new rapper trying to get on or someone asking for a job. I, on the other hand, was very laid back and low key. I stayed to myself most of the time but did make some friends along the way. I felt intimidated at times because everyone seemed to have money and the parking lot was full of luxury cars.

Some of the artists whose projects I can remember working on were jazz artist Jack McDuff, The Sugarhill Gang, West Street Mob, Sequence, Grandmaster Flash and the Furious Five, and the group Positive Force, to name a few. I would set up the tapes and take directions and of course mental notes from the engineer I was shadowing. His name was Billy Jones and I hung around Billy like flypaper. I wanted to know everything there was to know about being an engineer. There was a lot of time wasted as most musicians would tell you. No one ever got to the studio on time. However, the most important and organic relationship that was cultivated from the partnership with Sugarhill Gang, was between me and the Queen of Hip-Hop, Mrs. Sylvia Robinson.

Mrs. Robinson, after a few times of coming into the studio and calling the shots, giving her input, demands, and directions on how to modify the songs we were working on, started to take a liking to me. She would show up late at night to listen and then have us "fix it in the mix" as she would say. Then she would leave just as quickly, gracefully, and "bossfully" as she would come. She was all about business and perfection. She began to take me everywhere she went and had hoped to get me and her oldest son Joey to become best friends and comrades. I felt a bit intimidated because Joey had grown up as a rich kid. He had all the trinkets and toys that me and my hood kid friends couldn't afford. So, I felt like he was out of my league. Joey had a blue Mercedes and then a red Ferrari, not to mention the flyest gear in the neighborhood.

I have very fond memories of working with Mrs. Robinson and will always have a place in my heart for her and the education I gained from working with her. I can recall different incidents that happened that I will never forget. One such incident involved the famous Tito Puente.

## CHAPTER 5

# FOOT IN THE DOOR

I remember Tito Puente coming to record over the Sugar Hill tracks. I went to Newark (Club Paradiso) one night with Mrs. Robinson and it was there that the photographer shot the famous cover of the Sugarhill Gang. There were many nights like that, when Mrs. Robinson would take me with her to shows.

One night, we went to the famous club 2001 Odyssey in Brooklyn, where they filmed the dance scenes of Saturday Night Fever. It was always an adventure riding with the queen. I'm glad I took my camera with me back then because now I have the photos from our travels.

One day, as I sat outside of the studio, I looked up to see guys who had come from the "gutter" pulling up in brand new cars to grace the studio with their celebrity. They had made it, and I was still waiting to do the same. Scorpio had a brand-new maroon Mercedes, Melle Mel had a green Mercedes, Kid Creole had a black Audi, and Grandmaster Flash was flashy in his yellow L.T.D. Sugar Hill Records was the place to be. There was nothing but Rolls Royces, Ferraris, and Benzes in the parking lot and of course…my Toyota.

I created lasting bonds with many of the artists like Angie B of Sequence who would later become known as Angie Stone. The group Sequence had just arrived from South Carolina.

Blondy appeared to be the star of the group because of her popularity, and she stood out with the blond hair. Angie, on the other hand, was the songwriter and the voice of the group. Cheryl had charisma and seemed to hold her own.

*Sequence*

Then there was Grandmaster Flash, who I would go on to manage for over a decade. Looking back, Mel and Scorpio were always together so it's no surprise to see them performing together decades later. Now let me get back to the timeline.

I returned to college after losing it all, with the wherewithal to reinvent myself. In trying to recover from the loss of my equipment, and still find my path in music, I started attending concerts to stay in the music culture. One day on campus, I met a guy named Ed "Woodstock" Graves. It was 1981, and I had just pledged Omega Psi Phi. Ed, a fraternity brother, had started promoting concerts on campus and I approached him to work with him. He gave me a job as a roadie who would drive, set up equipment, and basically be the "runner" for what everyone who was someone needed or asked for. That was my introduction into the concert life.

During two concerts, I met Melba Moore and Phyllis Hyman, with whom I had an immediate connection. Melba had been to Richmond twice while I was working for Woodstock. At the time, Melba was a big star, and she was classy, funny, witty, and friendly. I loved watching her perform because she was a *real* performer. The second time I worked for her, I met Beau, Charles, and a road manager

*Woodstock & Mark Green*

named Bunky. Beau was demanding, and Bunky knew how to make it happen. After seeing my determination, drive, and passion, they were willing to help me in any way they could. I told Melba about my dreams and wanting to work for her, so she gave me her number and told me to contact her when I graduated. Phillis was another one who was a true performer. She did not hesitate to offer me her number as well.

As the end of my college life approached, I was chosen to be the Dean of Pledgees for my Omega Psi Phi family. It was the fall of 1983, and I was as happy as I could be because I had just finished school. However, I graduated with a Bachelor of Arts in Music Education and a minor in Communications.

I must say that pledging saved my life. Coming from the streets and having no discipline, I was buck wild! However, once I decided to pledge, I really got focused on school. First of all, you had to have a 3.5 grade point average and you had to find sponsors and really focus on the mission of the fraternity. After missing an opportunity to pledge in 1980 because I was not focused, I was devastated when I saw that line hit the block. It was something I wanted badly but I was too busy DJing and hanging out. The Spring '80 line set the standard for pledging. Those brothers were so tight and creative that everyone wanted to emulate them. It's funny looking back now forty years later, realizing some of my best friends are my frat brothers. We helped each other become men and we focused on uplifting, perseverance, and scholarship. It was the best decision I made while attending VSU. So many strong friendships grew from those relationships that I can't begin to thank all the brothers that have become part of my life. Rob Mason, my frat brother, and I became very close, and we still talk daily (*when he decides to pick up the phone*). However, the thing about Rob and I is that our school stories are similar in a way and we both graduated together which made it special.

After graduating, I looked for a job. The first position I landed was working as an apprentice engineer at Broccoli Rabe recording studio, where I got a chance to work on the famous wrestler, Sergeant Slaughter's, album. My dream was to return to Sugar Hill Records. However, right before I left, Mrs. Robinson hired a new young engineer by the name of Shameek. He and I did not really bond, and I saw that there was going to be some conflict, so I decide to spread my wings and see what else was available. I didn't want to burn that bridge, but little did I know that Sugar Hill would soon be shutting down.

During my transition, I decided to call Melba Moore. It was time to take her up on her offer. She set up a meeting and introduced me to Beau Huggins who gracefully invited me to become part of the Hush Productions team that he and Melba were running. Beau is the brother of Melba's then-husband, Charles Huggins. I had already been introduced to Beau in college, so the meeting was a positive one. We worked great as a team.

Bobby Duckett, another production guy, was making a name for himself in the entertainment industry. Bobby and I clicked from the beginning. We had great chemistry but every now and then, I would get upset with him and wanted to fight. We were like Heckle and Jeckle. Bobby had the gift of gab and a way of calming me down when I got to that point. We were assigned our first project which was to work with Lillo Thomas, the man known for "Sweet Surrender," "Sexy Girl," and "Good Girl." Lillo was a sex symbol at the time because he had that look that all the ladies liked and a smooth vocal sound.

One of our first shows was in Brooklyn. We were playing for a guy's wedding when we found out he was some gangster who was wanted by the FBI. During the wedding ceremony, he had his best man stand in for him to marry his wife. The FBI was standing all around waiting for him to appear. Now that was crazy!

I decided to take another job as well, working at the mall

managing a women's shoe store, to make ends meet. I really enjoyed the job and learning about women's shoes. We had four sales clerks, me, and the manager. During my time as a shoe store assistant manager, I noticed that at lunch time, everyone would stay on their lunch break and return sometimes even an hour after they should have come back. It was frustrating but the manager played a part in it as well. I had to get to the bottom of the unacceptable behavior. One day they let me in on the secret. Jack, one of my coworkers, invited me to the back and into their "secret society." Jack pulled out a little brown glass bottle that contained a white

*Lillo Thomas Band & Mark Green*

substance. I immediately knew that the substance was cocaine. Although I had never tried it before due to my athletic lifestyle, I was open to trying something new. Jack made it look so cool and inviting by the way he rolled up a dollar bill and tapped the container sprinkling the powder into lines on a table. The experience seemed harmless. He passed me the bill, I took a hit, and that was it. Little did I know, my life was about to take a drastic turn. I took that hit and felt an immediate rush of euphoria. It was like nothing was wrong and everything was beautiful. I didn't have a care in the world.

As weeks progressed, things in the store began falling apart. The "luncheons" began to take place daily and in exchange, my once progressive position became a mess. Money starting to turn up missing and shoes started walking out of the store on their own, and not in bags with paying customers. I decided to exit before I took a fall from grace and returned to working in the industry with Lillo. I did not, however, leave Jack. He became my main supplier. Cocaine was $100 for a gram, pure and uncut, which was expensive at the time. It was known as the rich people's drug but everyone in the hood made sure they found the money to be part of the society of affluent social indulgence.

Cocaine was not frowned upon but looked at as a way to party with a purpose. The purpose was to get high, have fun, and be free from your inhibitions. If you were subconscious about something, cocaine would help you throw care, concern, and caution to the wind. But that was the calm before the storm. It was a feeling that was unbelievable, and it made everything great. As I returned to work for Lillo, we began to do isolated dates. All along, that sensation stayed in my mind. Whenever I had extra time to myself, I would call Jack so I could get a hold of some happy powder. It was a pick me up and an escape from the rat race.

Within months, Lillo Thomas became the opening act for Eddie Murphy on his concert tour "Lawd Have Murphy," which would later be called the Raw Tour. I toured with Lillo as the drum roadie for Poogie Bell. I had no problem as the drum roadie because I played drums, and I knew how to play multiple instruments. Things were going great! I had never been on a tour bus. Every night we were in a different city and the excitement of riding on the bus and looking out the window as we traveled from state to state was exciting and new. We all had bunk beds so at any moment you would find yourself in your bunk reading or listing to music or just getting some rest. At times we would all be up in the front of the bus. Sometimes we would watch a movie together or put on music and sing along. The bus consisted of twelve beds and a master bedroom for the artist, and we had everything you can think of to make the trip comfortable.

Eddie was a major movie star and I was star struck when I

first met him. He'd just finished two movies and the Delirious Tour and was at the top of his game. He loved Lillo. There was no one bigger than him during the time. Lillo was also getting great recognition, because we were playing for a diverse audience, who really had no idea who he was, but they all loved him.

That's when I met Eddie's crew. There was Larry Johnson, Eddie's right-hand man, Federoff Colen, his stylist, Mark Cory, his other right hand and childhood friend, and Clint and Jerome. Months later there would be some other people joining us and they were all family members of Eddie—Ray Murphy, Charlie Murphy, and Uncle Ray.

Being on the Eddie Murphy tour opened many opportunities that I was not prepared for. I

*Larry Johnson & Mark Green*

remember going to the mall the first time with my laminate on and everywhere I went, people offered me discounts and free items. I was amazed at the response. Just meeting the people backstage was an adventure. Everyone from Willie Nelson, Prince, Stevie Wonder, Charlie Sheen, and more. I shared a room with Professor Griff of Public Enemy. However, the group had not debuted yet. I just knew him as one of Eddie's friends. We got along great, although he spent most of his time praying and practicing his martial arts. I, on the other hand, stayed up partying and hanging out each night.

While touring, I became aware, from my own experience of how a cocaine sniffer looked, of many others who were using that same powder to stay in a state of bliss. I got a great business idea. I got a half ounce from Jack on consignment and started my enterprise to supply and secure mine and other users' demands. It was great! I quickly returned his fee and increased my weight to one ounce. Eventually, other people caught on to what was happening. The big man himself wanted to know what was going on. He pulled me to the side one night and said, "Mark, why are people always looking for you after the show?" I didn't know what to say. But I did know my part-time job had to end. This was my first major tour and intro to the business, and I was determined to go all the way up. So, I gave up my part-time pharmaceutical gig and focused on touring.

Lillo left the tour during the second half and while he was gone, Eddie invited his childhood friend, Kenny, to open for him. He also asked me and Bobby Duckett to stay on and handle production for him. Well, that didn't last long. Kenny was the worst performer I had ever seen. He had a thing for Prince and would try to emulate him each night. He would come on stage and slide across the floor with a mannequin leg and pretend to lick it as he landed upstage with leg in hand. No one knew his music and it became a free for all in the audience. Word must have gotten out about his performance because by the third show, people brought tomatoes and started throwing them at Kenny along with other items. It wasn't long before Eddie's agent requested that he bring Lillo back.

About a week later, it was the culmination of the second half of the tour and everyone

*Mark Green & Bobby Duckett*

wanted to get their last party on. One of the band members invited me to his room to partake in some libations and while we were sitting there, he pulled out a bill with powder. He passed it to me, and I engaged in a homecoming event. My sweetie was back in my hands and took a trip from my nose canal to my brain. I felt good all over again.

I then asked him where I could get more product. He said to call his cousin JJ. When JJ arrived, he was a towering eight feet tall with a shoulder-length jheri curl, a fat gold chain, and some banging gear. He had a confident stroll and kept reminding me that he was from Oakland, California.

When I walked out the door, my eyes were wide. Not from the coke, but from the ride that JJ had. He had a Rolls Royce which was inviting. But his gold chain and jheri curl would have definitely put us in the line of "riding dirty" and being pulled over due to racial profiling. He assured me that he was clean and had no drugs on him.

We cruised in the Rolls to an apartment complex in South Central L.A. where I noticed two street security guards who were there to protect their illegal club that awaited our entrance. They had taken two apartments, combined them, and turned them into an after-hours spot. I was a little apprehensive because I was new to that hood and without the gear that matched my driver, I felt I stood out. I was not an OG. I had no rope chain on me, or the curly hair kit to match. I was the youngest one there and those guys were straight up gangsters.

As soon as I arrived with JJ, they opened the doors, and drinks, weed, and coke started flowing all around the room. The music was blasting and on the side of the wall was a pool table and some guys playing cards and rolling dice.

By 2:30 a.m. I was inebriated but not too drunk to notice an OG gangster chick eyeing me. She was about 5'5 and somewhere in her early forties. I was twenty-five and not checking for her, but I could tell that she'd been a hottie back in her day. I was high, but not high enough to be flattered or interested in her advances. She must have told some of the OG's that I was her target, because they were trying to push me onto her. Within thirty minutes, I was in the back of some OG's car and on my way to Long Beach, and ole girl's crib. No sooner than I was in her house, she rushed me to her bedroom and the next thing I knew, she was in the shower. I, on the other hand, passed out on her bed. Since I couldn't wait up for her to freshen up, I was awakened by slaps and pokes and remained on the living room couch with the order to "be gone by the time my kids get home." I was glad because I had no desire for ole girl.

I felt a frantic poking around 7 a.m. and before I could wash my face, I was put out onto the street, not having any idea where I was. The only directional advice I was given was that there was a bus stop on the corner. I got on the bus, and magically found my way back to L.A. I couldn't wait to get home with my horror stories, and back to my budding celebrity life. My roommate from the tour was worried about me and asked where I was and if everything was ok. I said yes and began to tell him about the crazy night.

About a week after we returned home, I was still enjoying the fact that I was slowly and surely becoming a part of Eddie Murphy's small clique. Eddie enjoyed throwing parties and I was invited to many of his functions by Federoff, his wardrobe stylist and Larry Johnson, his right-hand man. To whatever degree that I could, I would get in where I fit in. One time, when he had one of his shindigs, Eddie asked me to see if Lillo would collaborate with him on a song. Due to whatever other obligations Lillo had at the time, he could not commit. That is how Rick James came into play, and "Party All the Time" added to Eddie's resume. Although Eddie was having a great run as a standup comedian, he wanted to be a singer as well. He delegated the task of setting up his home studio to none other than the best—me. I was not only confident that I could do it, I assured him I could, until I saw a room full of equipment that had to be assembled. I humbly and suddenly found out that I was not the best. That gig was up when I had to confess that all I would do with that was create a mess. He may have never worked with me again and I wasn't going to lose that affiliation.

## Chapter 6

# PARTY ALL THE TIME

One New Year's Eve, Federoff invited me to Eddie's party. Although I had been to other events at Eddie's house, this one was "off the chain" as we used to say. The security was at an all-time high. You had to enter with invite in hand and you could not park on the property. They had a van that would escort you up from the street level to the top of Bubble Hill (Eddie's mansion). I guess because Red (my best friend) and I rolled up in a stretch limousine, they assumed we were important, so they let the car drop us off at the front door and no one asked for our invite. We walked in around 11:00 p.m. and lo and behold, there were people in

*Federoff Cohen*

every nook and cranny of the mansion and they were intent on trashing every corner. I was shocked to see the bathroom and other areas of the house looking like an overrun night club.

I was relieved and grateful when Federoff whisked me and my friend Red away to the VIP, with the real MVPs. There was Latoya and Janet Jackson, Stacy Latisaw, Mike Tyson, Arsenio Hall, Mustafa Farrakhan, and Sugar Ray Leonard among others. During that time, Red ran up to Latoya and started a conversation, but he kept mistaking her for Janet by addressing her as Janet, not recognizing that Janet was hiding in plain sight in the corner. I went over to steal a few moments of her seclusion and she was welcoming. We had a brief conversation in which I hit on her and gave her my number. I was so amped that she took my digits, but the next three days had me waiting for a call that never happened. I guess she didn't want to burst my bubble.

*Red*

I did get a chance to spend some time with LaToya after Red decided to chase after Janet. But we had a different conversation because I was in hustle mode. She had a record out at the time and was looking to go out on the road. I verbally ran off my resume and she was impressed and asked if I would mind setting up a meeting with her manager Jack. She kindly introduced us, and we decided to meet the next day at their hotel later in the evening. Of course, that never took place. As I sat in the lobby waiting on him, I began to feel like I had been bamboozled! After thirty minutes, it was a wrap for me. *(Rule #2: Don't Believe the Hype!)* Everyone has game in this business. The key is recognizing it before you get played. One thing I peeped on old Jack was that he seemed very controlling, which all makes sense because they later married. I guess he did not want me on the road with his future wife.

On another occasion at Eddie Murphy's house, I had brought my cousin Avis over to meet Eddie. She was so excited to be at his home and could not wait to meet him. As we sat in the dining area waiting for him to come down, this guy strolled in smoking a joint and the smell of it made me turn around quickly. As I looked in amazement, it was none other than Rick James. Before I could even introduce myself, he went directly to Avis, stuck his finger in his mouth, and placed

*Boogie Boys*

it on her lips and said, "I want some pussy tonight."

I was in shock! He totally ignored me, not caring if Avis was my girl or not. She, on the other hand, let out a short giggle and smiled. There were always celebrities showing up at Eddie's house, and I tried my best to stay connected.

As Eddie's tour came to an end, I was immediately hired

to manage a group called The Boogie Boys. They were only the third Hip-Hop group to be signed to a major label at the time, Capitol Records. The group consisted of Joe Malloy aka "Romeo JD," Rudy Sheriff aka "Little Raheim," and William Stroman aka "Boogie Nights," who missed out on the wave when he enlisted in the Army. Their hit song was "Fly Girl." The year was 1985 and I had begun having even better experiences, I cannot lie. Things were looking up. We were doing shows in small nightclubs, roller skating rinks, anywhere we could book a show. As a manager, I was no longer a roadie, I was the man. Part of my job was interacting with agents. I noticed that I wasn't the only one who had dabbled in narcotics. Managing Hip-Hop artists led me into the street world because rappers came from the streets where it was gritty and seedy. The culture was different from R&B. The promoters, managers, artists, groupies, etc. all had some connection to the hood, and it seemed like everyone was just a shady character trying to capitalize on the bridge between the music and the mayhem of everyday life in the city.

My passion and love for the industry was second to my love for the control that I had from knowing the artists and entertainers and having a say in their careers, even down to their itinerary.

Although Hip-Hop was in my heart and a part of my experience, I was a bit skeptical about working with unknown talent after working with so many big names. However, their talent and ability to take direction made me comfortable and I began to enjoy the fact that they were serious and disciplined. To them they weren't a fly by night group and they were determined to become a household name. Being the first rap group signed to Capitol Records was a major accomplishment that they did not take lightly.

*Boogie Boys*

As we began to book more and more shows, I realized that it was hard for these groups to get paid if they weren't the headliner or the opening act. Back then, you got paid after the show and a lot of janky promoters wouldn't even pay. Many artists would hit the stage, do their best, and be left hanging. It wasn't like today where everyone is getting the bag. They were left holding an empty one. So, I decided that my groups would be the opening acts if they weren't headlining, so we could be in and out although I didn't have any qualms about airing the place out if they played with our money. Fighting was never a fear of mine. I actually loved a good one.

# CHAPTER 7

# EMPIRE STATE OF MIND

I loved the Boogie Boys. Maybe because they were new to the game and I had the opportunity to school them. I loved that they had no problem taking direction and they respected my views and thoughts. It was an easy run and as we say, a match made in heaven.

One night, the Boogie Boys performed before I received the money. They had been told many times not to step one foot on any stage without my permission. I raised so much hell and blew my top that before I could say another word, Romeo JD had a new name for me. He got tired of my ranting and raving and said, "Ok, Mark Money Green." I liked it and that name would follow me through the rest of my career.

We were in Dayton, Ohio on another occasion and we were the first group to open the show. I went to get my money from the promoter, and I got way more than I bargained for. As I entered the promoter's office, I could tell that I was about to have a problem. The guy tried to diss me and tell me I wasn't getting paid before the show. That wasn't how I conducted business, and it wasn't going to start that day either.

I had a formula, and it was working. Before I could state my case, he pulled out a weapon and kept saying he didn't care if I was from New York, and at the time, I didn't either. I just wanted my payment.

The guy was not only brandishing a .357 magnum when it was all said and done, but I could tell that he was high as hell. He was a gangsta. He was not new to the streets and although the gun should have been enough to deter me from standing up for myself, I held my ground. Dude had the gun in my face, and he was not playing. I was stirred, not shaken. I knew I could take him out if I made the right move. He was about 5'8, stocky, but no muscle. I started thinking about how I was going to retrieve that gun from his hand but luckily, his partner came in yelling at him to put it away. It turned things around. But who knows how it would have gone down because one thing I was not going to do was let a clown play me just because I was in his town. *(Rule #6: It Ain't Where You From, It's Where You're At)*

Everyone wanted to talk about, "I'm from Brooklyn," "I'm from the Bronx," etc. But when you in another state, city, or country, no one cares because it ain't about where you're from, it's where you're at when shit is about to go down. This was a situation that would continue to repeat itself because as I explained, the streets and fame, in some areas, were one in the same. The element of music played not just in nice concert halls but run-down bars and clubs alike.

Some of the people that were touring with us were Divine Sounds, Joe Ski Love, The Real Roxanne, Lisa Lisa, Gordy's

Groove, Rapping Duke, Roxanne Shante, Sparkie D, Kool DJ Red Alert, and many more including UTFO whose lead singer was Kangol. Full Force was making a name for themselves, and we all were blowing up. While touring life was crazy, it was also fun. All the tour mates would become one big happy family and would play games and pranks on each other. One disgusting prank we would carry out was when some of them, not me ever, would pee in a garbage can, and then lean the garbage can against the door. We would then knock on the door and violate the poor soul who would open the door and be splashed with urine when they pulled the handle to open the door.

We were not only performing in concert halls and bars, but we even performed in barns. Yes, barns, like the ones that housed animals in big fields, where you expect everyone to have on overalls. That night was crazy. I remember all of us riding in two yellow school buses down some dirt road when we pulled up to the back of a farm inside a barn. They had people sitting around outside waiting for the concert to begin. At the end, there were no incidents, and everyone retuned back to the bus as we drove off to our hotel.

Another memorable experience was touring with the Fat Boys on their Swatch Watch Tour. I liked all of them but me and Prince Markie Dee, formed a special bond. We were inseparable and like two peas in a pod. After every show, we hung out until the wee hours of the morning. Someone today might say it was because we were light-skinned but I say it because he matched my cool. We had some great times that I will never forget. I was saddened, however, when I ran into him a while before he died, and he had no recollection of any of it. The memories still stay with me and in the words of Whodini's "One Love," RIP Prince Markie Dee. Your memory will forever live on in me.

One night I was with Buffy, the beatbox contender, and we had just come back from a show. I went into my hotel room and he went into his. His room was directly across from mine. About fifteen minutes later, I heard someone banging on another door outside in the hallway. I couldn't take the noise anymore so I swung my door open to get ready to give somebody the business. A girl was banging and crying on Buffy's door and as I tried to

*Buffy (Fat Boys)*

remedy the situation, she expressed through sobs that Buffy was in his room with another woman. She was crushed and I felt obligated to be a Good Samaritan.

I told the girl to wait in my room while I talked to Buffy. When he answered the door, he was sweating like a pig in grease and I was astonished by the sight of this 600-pound man and the nerve of him to try to wrap a towel around his waist. Once my shock subsided and I gathered my focus, Buffy confirmed her accusation. He confessed but urged me to convince her that he was not feeling well and wasn't up for company. That night, I carried out my sainthood and didn't pounce. She wasn't my type anyway...lol.

As that tour came to an end, we jumped on the Fresh Fest, which was Kurtis Blow, Divine Sounds, Whodini, Run DMC, Grandmaster Flash and the Furious Five, Jermaine Dupri, The Fat Boys, and The Dynamic Five. Me and X of Whodini hit it off and became brothers. Jermaine Dupri was fourteen years old at the time and was there because his dad was Michael Mauldin, one of the concert promoters. Jermaine was like the junior boss and was able to ride a moped across the stage during Whodini's set. Mopeds were new, and Jermaine had the world at his fingertips.

LL Cool J made a few appearances on some of our stops and let's just say, we were all "Fresh to Death." Young Black entrepreneurs, entertainers, tour managers, managers, and performers on down to gophers living out our dreams and paving our own way. Doing it like it had never been done before. Looking back, I wonder how we stayed on the road for so long making $1,500 a show. By the time the second record came out, we were up to $3,500 and that was considered a lot. We always traveled by plane. However, one time we had stayed up parting all night that by the time we got to the airport, we all fell asleep and missed our flight. I went and booked the next flight, and don't you know, we fell asleep again and missed that flight, too! I can't remember where we were going but we definitely missed two flights while already being at the airport.

As Hip-Hop accumulated more and more followers, we began to find ourselves on the west coast more than any other coast. I noticed that we were playing arenas and theaters, no more skating rinks and barns. The west coast really embraced Rap music. They were all about it and treated us like stars. One night in LA, we were on tour with some new west coast artist. People like Ice T and a guy named Rappin' Duke. I walked in the hotel lobby and saw these rappers in makeup with eyeliner and dressed like a rock group. I didn't know what to think. They were called The World Class Wreckin' Cru. Understand that we had no idea that the music we were making would change the world. For us it was all fun, like playing the dozens. We didn't realize its impact. We thought everyone was rapping but little did we know, we were laying the groundwork for a global culture.

Later that week, we had a show in San Bernardino, which appeared to be a quiet town like Sacramento, from what I remember. Unless we stayed in town for more than a day, it was hard to fixate on one town. It was all here today, gone tomorrow. We were playing an area, different from what we were used to. I spoke to the promoter about something, and she pointed to a light-skinned dude who was short and wearing a Kangol. He never smiled but seemed to be by himself at times. She immediately told me to stay away from him. So, I did and came to later find out his name was Ice T. While I was on tour, I stayed to myself and with my crew. LA was new to me and I had no desire to meet new folks. Staying away was a given.

*Rodney Gillison*

One day as I was driving and handling all the business of a road manager, I began to realize that driving was becoming too cumbersome and dangerous for me. I couldn't keep up my rigorous schedule of managing the artists and then keep my eyes open to drive at night. I contacted one of my old college music friends, Rodney Gillson, to be our driver. He, like myself, had dreams of making it big. Me and Rodney had the same undying passion for Jazz as I played the drums and he played the piano. We would spend hours in the rehearsal room at school working on our craft. However, those days were over and now we had to concentrate on our new gig. The Boogie Boys were becoming more and more known and noticed in Los Angeles. We were booking bigger and better venues. We gladly welcomed the arenas and said bye to the barns.

# CHAPTER 8

# ON THE ROAD AGAIN

After the Fresh Fest, I wanted to go in another direction and do something different. I remember constantly dealing with Mark Siegel, a booking agent at ICM agency. There was something cool about wearing a suit, carrying a briefcase, and having a big office overlooking the city. As a booking agent, we are responsible for finding work for the artists, like an employment agency. A manager handles the ins and outs of their group, and the tour manager handles all the managers of the artists while on tour. I had been a manager and tour manager up to that point. Now I turned my sights toward being an agent.

Being on the road was like going to a party every night in a different city. We were young and full of energy. What I noticed about touring different cities was that every city had its own slang, and it was amazing to hear some terminology from other places. Every now and then, we would pick it up and bring it back home. As we toured across the States, people outside of New York did not know what the term Fly Girl meant. Another one that sticks out is once when we were in

Ohio. They called women who were unattractive skeezers. It would be a year later that Kangol would record a song called Skeezer Pleaser that charted on the Billboard charts.

Before I could focus on becoming an agent, Hush Productions hit me up to be the road manager for Meli'sa Morgan. Her hit song "Do Me Baby" was out and she dressed, acted, and commanded the room like a real diva. Meli'sa was fine as hell and a straight up diva. She was demanding and knew how and what she wanted. Some people feared her, but I had to deal with her, and I did so cautiously.

Our first gig was a high school prom in Paterson, New Jersey. The promoter was Lamont Boles, who I would later work with in the music business. The next gig was at Delaware

*Mark Green & Mel'isa Morgan*

State and again, I was impressed with the promoter, Dave Wooley. He was not just a promoter but a gifted musician in his own right. He played the drums like no other and made me second guess my skills as a drummer. I truly admired him. As Meli'sa's song became more and more successful, there was no denying her talent. She had done well singing behind Chaka Khan but she truly stood out on her own and came out from Chaka's shadow to rise to the top of her game.

One night while in Mobile, Alabama for a show, Meli'sa forgot something in her hotel room. I rushed back to retrieve it and found myself without a fast enough way back. When I got to the lobby, I assumed that a certain gentleman was someone who worked at the hotel based on his attire. I frantically asked him if he would get me to the concert and he agreed. As we were driving and making small talk, I learned that the guy was at the hotel to try to meet his celebrity crush,

Meli'sa Morgan. I was so elated that I not only found a way back but could do him a solid by introducing him to her. My excitement turned to worry when he asked me to pass him a "package" out of the glove compartment. I obliged but then

*Fresh Fest Tour Jacket*

realized that it was cocaine, and I accidentally dropped the bag on his car floor. I was thought, *Oh shit, this guy is going to kill me.* Luckily, he didn't sweat it and told me to rub it into the carpet with my feet.

I had no inclination that he was a drug dealer, as I would later find out. He looked like a legitimate business man to me, although he said his name was School Boy. I should have guessed it because that is what he had on, schoolboy glasses. He wasn't your average drug dealer. He had on a three-piece suit and was not an attention seeker like some pharmaceutical dealers. He was classy, not flashy.

We had a great night and our meeting ended with an invitation to his Thanksgiving party the next day. On Thanksgiving Eve, I was excited and ready to party! However, I couldn't find anyone who wanted to accompany me to the dinner party. I couldn't quite understand how the band members, who were away from home, weren't interested in going. It turned out to be a blessing from God that kept me at the hotel because the next day I learned that School Boy had been murdered. His Thanksgiving dinner turned into a Last Supper because he was robbed and killed at his own event.

Meli'sa's "Do Me Baby" was climbing the charts to number one. Everything was great! Unfortunately, I had some issues with one of her band members. Sometimes on the road, everyone wants to be the boss. Meli'sa's right hand girl felt that her position called for her to call the shots or at least not have to listen to the shots I was calling. She was always trying to give me a hard time and had done it enough that I felt she needed to learn a lesson.

After numerous times of her being late, I decided to do something devious. I let the bus driver scare her into thinking she was getting left behind and asked him to pull off as soon as we saw her coming out the door. He pulled off as she ran out of the hotel. As she ran, waving and screaming, we all (the band) got a good laugh. The bus driver finally stopped the bus and let her on. Not only did she not like being the brunt of the joke, but she also took it upon herself to throw soda in my face. I immediately wanted to fight her because the anger between us had escalated over the weeks. Fortunately, I was grabbed by some of the band members and held until I cooled down. For some reason, I loved to fight, and I loved to fight people who underestimated me because I was quiet. Out of nowhere I would come out like a hurricane and just destroy everything in sight and that scared people. Let's just say that day she was lucky that I was raised to believe boys don't hit girls, and it was a way of life that I adhered to.

# CHAPTER 9

# OTHER SIDE OF THE RAINBOW

As the tour came to an end, I got a call from Kevin Harewood. Kevin was the Vice President and right-hand man to Melba Moore's husband, Charles Huggins. The call had me on edge initially because Charles was a no-nonsense type of guy, and I didn't want any conflicts. The call turned out to be a promotion to a full-time management position. Bobby Duckett and I had really begun to bond with our shows and our

*Kevin Harewood*

hard work made us the go-to people for road management and production. Our names were ringing bells on the tour circuit. Hush Productions was becoming like the new Motown and everyone on the label seemed to be blowing up in a big way.

At one of our meetings with Beau Huggins, he said, "I want to play you some new music by an up-and-coming artist named Freddie Jackson." I had met Beau when I was in college, and I felt comfortable being around him. At the time, I did not know his role at Hush. However, I soon found out he was the man who made everything turn to gold. When I heard "Rock Me Tonight," I knew it was a hit. Beau had an ear for good music and sitting in with him, grew my talent for the same. I was ecstatic about learning about songwriting and was interested in music production. Freddie was one of Melba's background singers who was ready to come to the forefront as a solo artist. The potential of being part of his transition into stardom put me on a natural high. I loved the process of making artists famous.

When I was in college, hearing Melba's song, "Other Side of the Rainbow" was one of my saving graces while going through tough times. I like to think that I was manifesting my future with her, every time I put that song on repeat, without knowing it at the time.

Being on the road with Melba Moore was the epitome of my dreams coming true. Melba was the queen with numerous hits, television shows, and films, and her choosing me to work with her was a badge of honor that I held

*Mark Green & Melba Moore*

dearly, like many of the plaques that I would eventually acquire for my walls. Melba was a star and she looked and acted the part. Everyone catered to her, and her company of artists began to blow up. She had her hands in everything, and she made sure it was a good look.

Fast forward to my meeting and finding out about working with Freddie Jackson. The elation was constant because Freddie would be one of my next projects and I was all in. I couldn't wait to work with him and express to him that with me, he was in good hands. The adrenaline rush of building and having a hand in growing talent was better than I could have ever imagined.

Another group that was coming down the pike for me to be involved in was Ray Goodman and Brown. They requested me and Bobby to handle their road management and productions. The year was 1986 and everything was going well. Their hit song "Take it to the Limit" was climbing the charts. Initially, they were called The Moments but due to legal issues, they had to change their name. The good thing was that it didn't stop their hits from rolling in and again, it was like a dream come true working with them as I had grown up listening to their music. When they say it's too good to be true, my life surely began to feel that way. Except it was too good, but actually true. This was happening and it was the moments like these that kept me hungry for more.

Harry Ray, the lead singer, had a soft falsetto voice like no other. Billy Brown, who was also a lead singer, sung one of my favorite songs, "Love on a Two-Way Street." Al Goodman, the baritone of the group, was the one with whom I was closest and had a friendship. We were doing theaters and clubs and

*Ray Goodman & Brown & Mark Green*

one night during a performance at Blues Alley, Washington D.C., they decided last minute to change their music set without my knowledge. As I listened, I was blown away that they were singing the songs that I loved. I went from their road manager, to short of a groupie when I heard "Gotta Find a Way," "Not on the Outside," "Just because He Wants to Make Love," and "If I Didn't Care." That was the first and last time I heard them sing their original classics. It was a once in a lifetime experience that still warms my heart to this day. I won't portray that everything was perfect or without challenges, because there were definitely trying times. But like anything else, you live and learn.

On one of our last tour dates, we ended up in Detroit, Michigan at a hood spot called Henry's Cocktail Lounge. It was like any other local bar where everyone knows everyone's name. As always, I would go to settle with the promoter before the show. Well on that night, I wasn't allocated the number of tickets that I needed for friends that I had invited to the show, so I snuck them in.

Henry was another old gangster that I nearly had a run-in with because when he found out I had snuck people in, he requested a meeting with me in his back office. My apprehension for performing in such a seedy place was confirmed because Henry invited his pistol to the conference and had me bound to a verbal agreement that I would pay for the people I snuck in, or he would have me brought out in a stretcher for the audience to see. I thought I was past the point of dealing with those type of people or having dangerous interactions, but the music business was still and will always be married to the streets. I did what any man who valued his life and his future would do. I paid.

As time passed by, we slowed down with our shows and things got a little complacent. I took on my next gig with Najee and while I was on the road, I got a disturbing call that Harry Ray had passed.

## CHAPTER 10

# IT'S SO HARD TO SAY GOODBYE TO YESTERDAY

Two of the saddest times in my life were missing Harry Ray's funeral while being on tour with Najee and the death of Al Goodman. Harry was a classy singer. He looked the part and all the ladies loved him. He was cool as shit and we got along great. I was shocked by his death and to be honest, I still don't know what happened. No one really talked about it. So, we took Ice, who was the background singer, and brought him up front to replace Harry Ray because...*the show must go on*.

Al Goodman had remained my friend for many years after our working relationship ended. Al and I met early on back when Sugar Hill was called All Platinum Records. I was young and thirsty wanting to do anything I could in this business and Al would take the time to speak with me. It wasn't until years later that I got an internship with Sugar Hill that I was able to see Al on a regular basis and he would always give me sound advice.

Many years later, I saw Al in church one Sunday and he

told me that he had to have surgery. He expressed that he was anxious about it and concerned. Although he mentioned it casually, I could sense that he was troubled. I brushed it off because I didn't want to give negative energy to his worry. I didn't want to believe that anything bad would happen and told him not to worry about it, that he would be fine. I assured him that I would keep him in prayers. That was the last time I spoke to him as he died in surgery the very next day.

That day hurt. All I could think of was what I could have done to make him feel comfortable or what I should have said. I just felt so bad about the whole ordeal. I immediately arranged his funeral to be held at the Bergen Performing Arts Center, in Englewood, where he resided for many years. I was elated to help and bring his close friends like Millie Jackson, William "Poogie" Hart from the Delfonics, and Melba Moore together. It was my last gesture as his friend to send him off like a star.

By then, Hush Productions was the company that everyone wanted to join. I worked with some good people whose names I cannot leave out. Jackie Rhinehart, Andre Thorpe, Virgil Thompson, Von Alexander, and Derick Lewis were employees of Hush who went on to positions at Universal Music and other companies. Their careers started with Hush and they went on to do great things behind the scenes in the industry.

It seemed like every time I came back to Hush, there were new employees, as the company grew larger and larger. Beau invited me and Bobby to his office one day and I felt like I was going to see the Wizard. His office had a magical ambience as he would play music and have the lights down low to create a sense of euphoria and a calming peace. It was like going to see a musical guru. Beau put on a record by an artist named Najee which was a cover of Anita Baker's "Sweet Love." The melodic dance of Najee's saxophone to the very successful chart-topping hit by Miss Baker was quite soothing. But releasing two versions of the same song at the same time seemed, to me, a risky move. But Beau knew a hit when he heard one and although it was not common practice to do such a thing, it ended up being a win.

Najee's instrumental rendition of "Sweet Love" climbed the charts and landed in the Top 5 of the R&B charts and birthed the "Smooth Jazz" category. He was the catalyst to create that new genre.

The next stop for me was Florida on Najee's tour. Jackie Rhinehart had come

*Najee & Mark Green*

on the scene just as we signed Najee. Jackie had the gift of gab and her marketing ideas were needed at Hush. She had that persuading and convincing gift as well. She knew how to find the rough diamond in all the artists and would groom and polish them enough to turn them into shining stars. Everyone wanted to be down with us, and we were becoming the talk of the town.

One day while visiting ICM's agent, Mark Seigel's office, I noticed that he always had on a suit and carried a briefcase. He basically looked like a professional businessman, and I wanted to continue into a corporate position as opposed to continuing to be involved in parties and bullshit. He also had a bunch of gold record plaques on his wall, and I was determined to step into that world.

My first notion was to become an agent and book nothing but rap artists. By 1986, Rap music started falling out the sky like raindrops. Record companies had no idea what to do with it or how to sell it. It was an underground trend that was cornering the market. I remember when I managed Boogie Boys opening for Cameo, Morris Day and the Time, and many big headliners. They all hated us and our music.

I knew that Rap was going to get bigger, and I could make a name for myself because I already knew all of the Hip-Hop artists. Plus, what artist doesn't want to be booked for shows? None.

## CHAPTER 11

# SECRET AGENT

As I began to research the booking agencies, I came across ABC, Associated Booking Company. I heard about an opening and applied. Within the same day, I was called in by Oscar Cohen, an OG in his own right. Oscar was sharp and immaculate. He was groomed from the well-laid hairs on his head to his manicured and clearly polished fingernails. Every day of the week he looked like Al Pacino or Robert DeNiro in one of their gangster roles.

During the interview, Oscar sat me down and asked if I knew anything about the theatrical business, which I didn't. He was adamant about letting me know that the opportunities he could give me would be endless but not without my blood, sweat, and tears making me deserving of it. He said, "You're a good-looking kid and I'm not bringing you in here to be a "house nigger." I had to keep my mouth from dropping to the floor because I wanted the job. However, in the back of my mind I was thinking, *what did he just say to me?*

I took the position with ABC and left my position at Hush Productions, because I saw it as my chance to become a powerful agent. At the time, I was the only Black person at the company but that never crossed my mind because we were selling Black music and that's all I cared about. Well, that and making a name for myself. I continued to listen to Oscar and watched every move he made. I kept my eye on everyone there. I had a big office overlooking Manhattan on 66th and

*Toby Ludwig, Oscar Cohen & Mark Green*

Broadway. I was called to my first meeting to discuss the Anita Baker Tour and at that meeting, I met Toby Ludwig. We were newbies at the company and formed a tight bond that is still strong to this day. During the meeting, we were presented with the Anita Baker Tour and at the time, she was making $2,500 a show as her album "Rapture." The single, "Sweet Love," was making her a star.

We were delegated territories to sell our shows to and for some reason, I oversaw states where I wouldn't expect many to want to see Anita Baker, or any other Black artist for that matter, let alone know who she was. I was shocked to see my roster of states included Nebraska, Oklahoma, Tennessee, Iowa, and Kansas, to name a few. *How on earth was I going to book a concert in those places?* I thought.

During the meeting, we were told that there was going to

be a Black promoter by the name of John Ray who was put in charge of Anita Baker's tour. Oscar mentioned that he needed a Black promoter to take over the tour because she was an unknown artist, and it was going to be hard to get it done. So, Oscar felt John would be best for the job.

After we sat down and listened to the album, I knew Anita Baker was going to be the next big thing in music. We decided to sell her at ten thousand dollars per show, which today would be fifty thousand. That was big bucks back then!

I was having a hard time selling her shows in my lily-white territories, so I started calling old college buddies, those with capital of course, like Jay and Terry. I met Jay and Terry while attending VSU. They both lived in an affluent town in Maryland and came from money. Terry and Jay were best friends who live around the corner from each other. Terry and I formed a lasting relationship during my last years at VSU and Jay and I had been friends since our freshman year.

Terry had already had his hand in promoting concerts. They lived in the D.C. area, which wasn't my territory but known for jazz, and I knew I just needed to book a few shows in familiar places to have the momentum continue.

I convinced my "brothers" to put up the money. It took hours for me to convince them to give ten thousand each to finance two shows. They were hemming and hawing the whole day, and I was beyond frustrated when they took up my entire day only to leave me empty-handed. Oscar was furious and came down hard on me for not getting the deal done.

On many occasions, Oscar would intimidate the staff by

patrolling outside of everyone's office, pacing and spying on our meetings and listening to our calls and conversations. He had no shame or filter, as they say today, and would call out infractions while we were on the phone. If we were having a phone conference, he would butt in if he heard us say something wrong, with no regard to its inappropriateness. I felt like a goldfish that was thrown in the ocean and surrounded by a huge shark. It was intimidating and nerve wracking.

As I think about the documentary, *The Black Godfather,* I think of Oscar, who was in the movie. He took the playbook right from his boss, Joe Glazier, who was the right-hand man to Al Capone. One day we had a show in East Orange and as always, Oscar would take us out to eat before the show. On that day, one of the agents asked for a vodka and tonic and the bartender told him they didn't have any more vodka. Well, that did not sit well with Oscar. He said, "What kinda fucking place is this?" He took a twenty dollar bill out of his pocket, crumbled it up, and threw it in the face of the bartender. "Go to the fucking store and buy some fucking vodka." Oscar did not take shit from anyone and lived up to that gangster lifestyle. I loved that about him.

Part of my duties as an agent was to work in the mail room. Toby and I would spend time there, and I would enlighten him on who the Black artists were and we would discuss strategies on how to sell better and make more money. Every day we would have lunch together. We considered our meetings "power lunches" although they included $1.99

chicken salads or two hotdogs and a drink for $2.00 at Gray's Papaya on 72nd Street. It was all we could afford.

One of the things I didn't like about the job was having to hand deliver contracts to the artists. Toby and I would take turns delivering them. I would always visit Phyllis Hyman, Lionel Hampton, and one of Oscar's close friends, George Wein, the creator of the Newport Jazz Festival. Oscar would get a kick out of telling me that George was married to a Black woman. Back then it was rare or rarely seen. He also liked to tell stories about Billie Holiday, Sarah Vaughn, and Louis Armstrong. His stories were always entertaining, especially the ones about Joe Glazer.

Joe Glazer ran all Al Capone's speakeasies. During that time, Joe was feared by many because of his mafia connections. He was run out of the club business by law enforcement and decided to get into management by managing Louis Armstrong. He hired Oscar to be the road manager for Mr. Armstrong. When Joe died, he (allegedly) left ABC to Oscar.

The day we signed one of my favorite artists, Dennis Edwards, the lead singer for the Temptations, I felt like a winner. When "Don't Look Any Further" came out, we were all feeling like we couldn't be stopped. However, Dennis had run into some personal issues that he was trying to

*Dennis Edwards & Mark Green*

work out. This led to him calling the office for advances on his money, more times than Oscar cared to accept. During his challenges, Toby and Dennis bonded and became close. They kept that bond for many years and Toby actually became Dennis' manager when Dennis reunited with the Temptations prior to his death. I, too, ended up working with him years later as his agent. Three of my most memorable and favorite events working with Dennis were having him perform for 50 Cent's grandparents' fiftieth anniversary party, booking him

*(Top) 50 Cent & Mark Green;*
*(Bottom) 50 Cent & Dennis Edwards's Temptations*

to sing at a New Jersey Nets game, and lastly, experiencing him singing for South Africa's President, Jacob Zuma's birthday party in Washington, D.C. These were all star-studded events.

I was afforded the opportunity to sit down one day with

Dennis regarding the making of his songs and I was eager to know if that famous line in "Papa was a Rolling Stone" was true about his father. Everyone knows the start of the song and how it goes. "It was the third of September, the day I'll always will remember. That was the day that my daddy died." It was touching to know that the line was about his father who had died on the third of October. But it was even more refreshing to find out that he had not been a "rolling stone" but actually a preacher. No one ever would have expected that, as that song was so relatable and believable for many whose fathers were always bouncing in and out of their lives. However, Dennis and I would go on to be good friends all the way up until his death.

Many days, I would stand in my suit and gaze out of my office window and see my briefcase, which housed my pay stubs which reminded me that I was only making $250 a week with a take home pay of $187.50 after taxes. It was humbling, to put in nicely. I was discouraged and had not imagined in a million years that this is where I would be financially, especially not working in a high-rise on Broadway. My dream had become a sad song.

Things began to look up as I did not give up and instead booked Bobby Bland, BB King, Roy Ayers, and Lonnie Liston Smith. After bringing in a certain amount of income, I mustered up the courage to tell Oscar that I was considering leaving. He thought that offering me another fifty dollars a week would suffice. I was bummed out. I had made way more money at Hush Productions, but I took the raise and continued to work there for a short period of time.

## CHAPTER 12

# MICROPHONE FIEND

I was getting frustrated and wanted to go back to my roots, my original entry into the biz—Hip-Hop. I decided to reach out to some of my friends from the tour and sign some of those guys to ABC. The first person I called was Tyrone Williams who owned Cold Chillin' Records.

Tyrone was amped to hear from me and gave me Roxanne Shante and MC Shan. He started telling me about another new kid named Biz Markie but I turned away from it to focus on my two new artists. I also heard about two rappers from Philly that were making a buzz.

I went to Philadelphia and met with the Hill Top Hustlers. They were brothers by the name of Dana and Lawrence Goodman. They were

*Fresh Prince, Mark Green, and Jazzy Jeff*

managing The Fresh Prince and DJ Jazzy Jeff, who released their first song titled, "Girls Ain't Nothing but Trouble." After hearing the song, I took the record to the Mr. Magic show on WBLS and the rest is history. It was 1986 and Will Smith had just graduated from high school. I booked his first show at the world-famous Latin Quarters. That club was the place to be for all the soon-to-be famous, up and coming, and already successful rappers. Will was nervous, but I told him that he

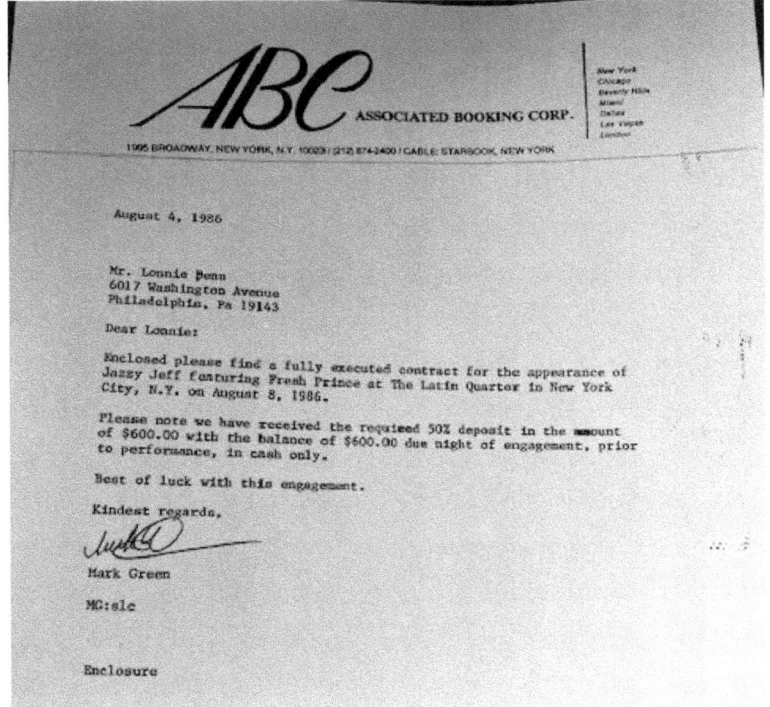

would do great. I don't remember a lot about that night other than being in the dressing room and the folks screaming and yelling, loving the performance. There was something about Will and Jeff that kept me hungry. I liked their style and was eager to take them to the top.

I went from feeling down and out, to feeling like The Man. The next artist I signed came from a guy out of Queens who was managing and producing a few artists. His name was Herby Luv Bug and he had me book shows for Salt-N-Pepa and Kid 'n Play. Then I signed The Skinny Boys. I was on a roll but back then the artists were only making $1,500 to $3,500 a show, which means I was only making a commission of $150 to $350 for all the work, running around, and politicin' aka, making power moves. Again, I was running out of steam.

During that era, there was no other producer bigger than Herby. He had a label, artists, and he was killin' the game. We developed a friendship, and he kept me fresh.

Later, I signed two singers named Two Tons of Fun who were renamed The Weather Girls. One of the things that Oscar taught us was that we had to always attend the shows of the artists that we booked. I felt important being the head of the entourage. I booked The Weather Girls at the Garage, a gay club. The Garage was the biggest club in NY at the time and performing there was a badge of honor. At the time, I didn't feel comfortable being seen there. Although I have no problem with homosexuals, I did have a problem being mistaken for one. It was my first time in a gay club and seeing "hard rocks" or B-boys in the club showing public displays of affection. I was shocked to see them holding hands. I was naïve to think the gay community only looked a certain way or behaved in a certain way. It was eye opening and educational.

I respected the phrase "to each his own" even more because no matter how people may have been uncomfortable with their perceived flamboyance, they were people just like everyone else. People who loved good music and having a great time listening to it.

On that night, we were preparing for the show and as I entered the dressing room, I found that the girls were still getting dressed. Man, I had never seen a bra that big! Lol! Then I had to go to the bathroom, but I was shook. I was afraid to go in because it was gay night and I had no idea what was going to happen. I got in and got out but kept my eyes on my surroundings. Then I decided to see what was going on upstairs and that was when I saw two B-boys with Cortefiel coats on and Timbs holding hands. It blew my mind. Finally, it was showtime and guess what song they sung? "It's Raining Men."

I was feeling back on top as I signed several more Hip-Hop artists, including Rainey Davis, whose hit was "Sweetheart," a dancehall artist, jazz artist Mike Stern, and many others. Although business was consistent, Oscar wasn't impressed. He loved the fact that I was bringing money in, but he wasn't delighted about the talent I was signing. Oscar was my mentor, and I appreciated the opportunities that he had given me, but in my gut, I knew our working relationship was becoming strained and approaching its end. We had a good run but dealing with him was no longer fun. I give him credit for being a crude businessman, but music is entertainment and he made it more of a job, than an adventure. I had gotten into the business because I loved it. I had gotten into it for the thrills and although I wanted money, I wanted to be free to enjoy my career that was my passion.

One day, as I spoke with Oscar, he told me I could only sell to three Black promoters—Bill Washington, Al Haymon, and John Ray. Al Haymon was the biggest promoter of his time and created the Budweiser Superfest concert series. Sometime after that meeting with Oscar, I got a call from a promoter in Connecticut who talked about booking a Hip-Hop show. Although the words of Oscar rang in my head, as soon as the phone rang, I was determined to prove Oscar wrong. I ended up selling the Black promoter in Connecticut a show. As the days got closer, there was no deposit. I began to get angry but now I was too far in to pull out so I ended up having to pay out of my own pocket because I could not go back to Oscar to explain my situation. The show was a success, but I never got the money until…

Years later he became a big-time promoter booking major headliners. He didn't know I was the tour manager for one of his upcoming shows. He was very surprised to see me but even more surprised about my actions. I was determined to get my money. When we got to the venue, I asked him about the money and he tried to play me. So, I decided to play him back. I told the artist that I had not received the money and that we could not go on. They were fine with it. The promoter wasn't. He started pressing me as the crowd grew impatient. Once they started chanting, he was about ready to beg. He needed us to go on and not ruin his image and I needed my money. I held up his show for more than an hour, until he paid me back the money he owed me. Oscar had warned me about dealing with "janky" promoters because he knew the business. Ultimately, it taught me a lesson. Although I was ready to move on, what he instilled in me I am still grateful for. *(Rule #5: C.R.E.A.M.)*

**Cash Rules Everything Around Me.**
**Get the money.**

Oscar came into my office and said, "I'm tired of you booking Shitty Shit and Shabby Shab (he was talking about Jazzy Jeff and the Fresh Prince). You better book some BB King and Bobby Blue Bland or your ass is going to be out of here!"

## CHAPTER 13

# ROCK ME TONIGHT

After Oscar said that I knew that was my queue to start packing. I let him know I was ready, willing, and able to go back to Hush Productions. I immediately called Charles Huggins expecting him to accept me back with open arms, but he had another idea. Charles wanted me to stay in booking, so he would have someone on the inside in place to keep an upper hand in controlling the Black music department at the world-famous William Morris Agency. Working for that agency sounded inviting as they were reputable and successful, but my balloon popped very quickly. Here I was with all these experiences, had all these great shows under my belt, and where did the agency put me? Right back in the damn

*Charles Huggins & Mark Green*

mailroom! I wasn't a rookie anymore. This wasn't at all called for. I was disappointed and fed up. They tried to tell me I had to work my way up. I was already up!

When I was asked if I would move to L.A., I told myself no way! Enough was enough. I vented to Charles and he finally gave in and welcomed me back. When I returned to Hush, so much had changed. They had signed Kenny G, Kashif, and actor Tom Cruise.

My first assignment was to manage the Force MDs tour. I jumped right on it, and it was like riding a bike. I hadn't missed a beat. I was their road manager and we were the opening act for New Edition's "All for Love" tour. That was a hot ticket and we felt hotter than fish in grease!

When I look back now, I laugh at the fact that the tickets were only eight dollars and fifty cents. The Force MDs were climbing the charts with "Tender Love," "Itchin for a Scratch," "Tears," "Let me Love You," and "Love is a House." They were extraordinarily talented. They did back flips, back spins, break dancing, and they gave New Edition a run for their money. They could have easily headlined the show. It was great working with the Force MDs every night. They gave a great show and would bring the house down. I really had no relationship with New Edition because they were always secluded. However, New Edition and Force MDs remain friends up until today.

After the first weekend, I was called back into the office for Bobby and me to meet with Beau. Freddie's song, "Rock Me Tonight" had already made it to number one. They decided to put out a couple more singles and get geared up for his "Tasty Love" tour. Our challenge was to put together an extraordinary band who would make this tour out of this world. We came up with Poogie Bell, Vincent Henry, Mike Campbell, Cindy Mizell, Audrey Wheeler, and Artie Reynolds. These were respected names and musicians, but we needed a keyboard player. We enlisted a Swiss musician whose distinguished accent made him stand out. His look was that of a classical pianist. We listened to his tracks and imagined him headlining one day because he was just that talented. His name was Alex Bugnon. As we prepared for the tour, I had to run to FedEx to send out some

*Mark Green & Freddie Jackson*

paperwork. While there, I met a young lady at the counter. She was cute with short hair and a slim figure. I started flirting with her and we exchanged numbers. We started spending time together and as the days went by, I found myself spending more and more time with her. She was highly intelligent and loved to read. Her name was Victoria and she lived in the Bronx. We began to date seriously and after six months, Victoria told me she was pregnant. I was devastated and did not know what to do. All I knew was I was not ready for fatherhood. I was more concerned about my career. The thought of being a father was unimaginable. However, during this same time, Bobby informed me that his girlfriend was pregnant too. It was comforting to know we were both about to hit the tour and we both had buns in the oven. Although Bobby's words and actions calmed me on the outside, I was still devastated inside. I had just begun to discover my career and learn about the industry. *How can I be a father now?* As it got closer to the birth of our daughter, Victoria and I began to have issues. Mainly because of my lifestyle and my partying habits. We both had our own names for our daughter and could not come to an agreement when suddenly, a nurse said, "What about "Renee?" A light hit me…Janay! That was the name of one of Freddie Jackson's songs and it had meaning to both of us since we met when I started touring with him. So, we looked at each other and agreed! Janay Imani Green was born!

The band was now complete and we were ready to go. As we gathered on the tour bus heading to our first show, my head was back in the clouds. I was the tour accountant and the tour manager, along with my friend Bobby Duckett. Bobby handled production, I handled the tour, and Andre Thorpe was Freddie's personal assistant. Our first stop was Detroit, Michigan. As I walked into the arena, I ran into a guy who is still my friend, NBA All-Star and basketball legend, John Salley. We immediately connected and I gave him some tickets to the show. Although I knew I was not a newbie, I was in awe that I was in charge of the 19,000-seat venue, The Palace of Auburn Hill arena.

The Tasty Love tour began with LeVert as the opening act

and then Meli'sa Morgan performed before Freddie headlined the show. It was such a good show and I loved it so much that I would watch the whole show. I didn't always watch the opening acts, but I had become close to Gerald and his group, LeVert. They were more than just an opening act, they were truly stars in the making. How could they

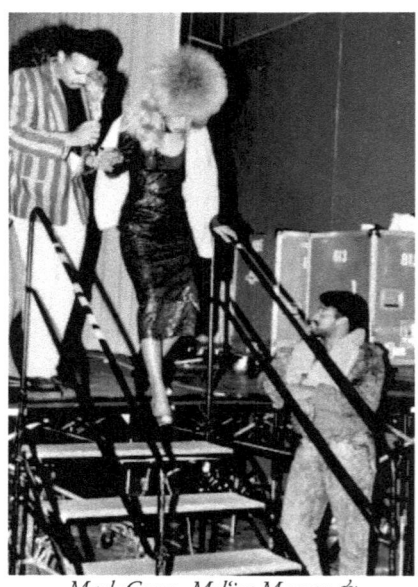

*Mark Green, Mel'isa Morgan & Gerald LeVert*

not be with Eddie Levert Sr. of the O'Jays as their dad? When Meli'sa came out, her energy and performance took the crowd's excitement and participation up another notch. Her voice was strong and powerful and the way she sung would make any man fall to their knees.

Now it was Freddie's turn. The music from the song "We Gonna Have a Funky Good Time" by James Brown cranked out of the speakers as Bobby, "The Voice of God," announced Freddie Jackson's name and he sauntered down a white staircase. The crowd broke into a frenzy. This type of behavior happened nightly with the crowd growing bigger and stronger. Every night the show got better and the word on the street was he was neck and neck with Luther Vandross.

## CHAPTER 14

# JUST A FRIEND

We had just played Cleveland, Ohio when someone from the band brought a girl on the bus. This was not uncommon during a tour as groupies always seemed to find their way backstage or into someone's bedroom. After day two on the road, I noticed the girl had on the same clothes and had no luggage. I approached her about her date and which person was responsible for her being there, but she refused to acknowledge the person. So, I gave some money to one of the female band members and asked her to go to the store and buy her a toothbrush, underwear, and any other essentials that she may need. By day four it was time for the chick to bounce. Since no one wanted to claim her, I asked all the band members for a couple of dollars to send her on her way. No one refused and I gathered the collection. I asked the bus driver to drive us to the nearest bus station and unbeknownst to her, I went in and bought a one-way ticket back to Cleveland. I then gave her a handful of money and sent her on her way.

I had to always stay on top of what was happening because as a boss, you are the most hated and least liked and everyone wanted to challenge you at times. People soon realized that game recognize game and I was not the one to play with.

During the trip, I was reflecting on my life and life on the road. There were many times on the tour bus that I would gaze out of the window and feel so fulfilled. It never got boring, and it was always a different experience, a different adventure. Before working in the industry, I had never been to most of the states but now, I had a first-hand experience in many.

There were days when everyone would hang out, watch movies, and talk about everything under the sun while having a great deal of fun. And then there were times when everyone would retreat and be in their own zone. There was the former, the latter, and everything in between. I continued to want to pinch myself although I knew that my life was just a dream, not a nightmare. I was content with tour life. I saw it as fun, lucrative, and I would not trade it for the world. I was definitely "about that life."

Miami was the ultimate party and Freddie loved it as much as Miami loved him. By now, the tour lineup had changed to Ray Goodman and Brown, Meli'sa Morgan, and Najee. Freddie got along with everyone, and he really enjoyed the super stardom that caused everyone to want to bow at his feet. Freddie truly had a good run as the "King of R&B" during his reign. Luther Vandross was another R&B King and Freddie was giving him a run for his money, as they were running neck and neck in success.

Every night after the show, Bobby and I would meet up to discuss the show and figure out how to make it better or fix what may have gone wrong. We would plan the next day and finish up the night with drinks. We truly were our brother's keeper and Beau would always remind me to watch out for Bobby which I always did.

One night after our show in Miami, we met a very pretty tall, light-skinned, model type girl, and Bobby and Andre brought her backstage. Her appearance had everyone in awe. One person in particular could not get over her. He was infatuated the first time he saw her and the next thing we knew, she was in NY in a Freddie Jackson video playing his love interest. As the songs grew and the video got bigger, Michael Michele was on her way to stardom.

Eventually, she landed a role in New Jack City as the love interest of Christopher Williams and has since gone on to act in movies and various shows.

Things were moving fast and part of my day job was to work on the video edits of Freddie's and Meli'sa's videos when I was not on the road. I was also in charge of casting which is something I truly adored. I learned so much about editing that I actually considered it as a career. I was amazed how you could change the colors of the cars, and make them go fast or slow. We could make it rain or make it sunny and we could also shave some weight off of someone, if needed. It was all so fascinating to me.

The following week I was back on the road headed to Dallas, Tennessee, Charlotte, and Chicago. It was so exciting because I had never been to any of those places. When we arrived in Dallas, I immediately went and got something to eat. I was extremely ecstatic about being in Dallas, having thought about visiting that city one day. I remembered that JFK was assassinated there and thought back to the announcement on the news as a young boy. As we traveled throughout the Midwest, we saw signs offering money to people for moving into an apartment. I had never seen anything like that coming from NYC. I had always wanted to visit Dallas. But unfortunately, my first encounter was a negative one.

## CHAPTER 15

# STOP, LOOK, LISTEN TO YOUR HEART

While sitting in the restaurant, I realized I was the only Black person there but it did not seem like it mattered. As I waited, the waitress, an old lady who was about eighty years old, or at least looked like it, rudely informed me that, "We don't serve your kind here."

I looked at her and I politely left not wanting to start any commotion and end up like Emmett Till or countless other people who went south and never made it back home alive. I quietly walked out being stunned that this was still happening in the United States of America in the 1980s. It was traumatizing, as that was my first-time touring across the country and seeing the parts I'd only heard or read about.

As we left Dallas on our way to Tennessee, one of the roadies pulled me to the side to tell me he thought he left Freddie Jackson's wardrobe box at the venue in Dallas. I was totally shocked and angry. I sat there for a moment to think about how and what we were going to do. I couldn't tell Freddie and there was no time to hire a tailor so I asked the bus driver to stop the bus. I went in my briefcase and gave the roadie $500. I told him to get off the bus, take Mitch with him, and to rent a van to drive back to Dallas and get the wardrobe box. They could meet us in Tennessee. I told both of them if they were not back by showtime, not to come back at all!

Hours later, we drove into Knoxville, another city I was entering for the first time. As we pulled into the rest stop, I asked an older white man, "Where is there to go around here?" and his response was out of a "Texas Chainsaw Massacre" movie. He said, "There's places you can go, and places we ain't gon' let you go." On that note, I returned to the bus and we kept it pushing.

We got to the venue and with a bit of surprise, the guys made it back in time for the show. That was one moment that had me sweating all day. I could not imagine telling Freddie he had no clothes for the show.

Tennessee was scary to me. It appeared everyone was a member of the Klan. I remember in Nashville, me and two other band members made our way to a club. When we walked in, it seemed like the music stopped and everyone just stared in disbelief. As soon as we entered, everyone turned around, surprised to see the two of us standing there. We turned around and closed that door just as fast as we opened it.

Charlotte, North Carolina was up next and what happened there is not even perceptible to the imagination. It was worse than a horror movie idea. It had to be about 11 am in downtown Charlotte when we ran right smack into a Ku Klux Klan march. I could not believe what I was seeing. I felt like I was in a movie from the 1950s. As the hooded men passed in front of the bus, all I could think about was grabbing a gun because I feared for my life. I think we all looked like our eyes were bulging out of our heads because no one could believe what their eyes were seeing. As the Klan walked past the bus, I instructed the driver to do his best to get us out of the city without running anyone over. That was one sight I can never get out of my head.

Chicago was our next destination. I figured it couldn't possibly get worse. I should have reconsidered that though because we had to travel back through Tennessee to get to Chicago. We were making our way through the Blue Ridge Mountains late at night and the bus was quiet as everyone was sleeping. I was awake listening to music and reading a book when the bus started swerving. Normally, there was always someone to stay up to keep the bus driver alert. That night that wasn't the case so I made my way to see if the driver was okay and he was not okay. When I pulled back the curtain I saw why. He was trying to light a crack pipe! This dude was smoking crack while driving a bus in the mountains, along narrow curves and a winding trail!

Let's just say that when I pulled back the curtain, saw him with the pipe, I blacked the fuck out like anyone would have.

I yelled, "Motherfucker, what are you doing! You trying to kill us? Put that shit away and drive to the next truck stop!"

I sat in the passenger seat looking out the window as we drove through the mountains. All I could see and imagine was the bus plunging 1000 feet down the embankment. I was praying to God to please just get us safely to the truck stop. I let him know that he would not be accompanying us anywhere else but there. He stopped at the next bus stop but it was still nighttime, so I called the owner of the bus company. The owner told us to stay put for the night and he would have someone else there to continue the job in the morning. Although it wasn't another encounter with racism, the whole trip was filled with near death experiences.

When the new bus driver arrived, I told the rest of the crew on the bus what had happened the night before. I didn't wake anyone up because I didn't want to give them the same anxiety that I was feeling after knowing that the guy was high on crack and driving us through a dangerous route. Who knows what one of them would have done and fighting while driving, smoking crack, and being in the mountains just didn't mix. I handled it myself and prayed the whole time. I had never been so happy to make it to a bus stop before in my entire life.

## CHAPTER 16

# GET THE STRAP

We arrived in Chicago on the tour bus as everyone else flew into the city. We had an extensive guest list and all of the executives from Hush were arriving along with Jesse Jackson, Louis Farrakhan, executives from Ebony and Jet magazines, Oprah Winfrey, and a host of others who are in the Who's Who of Entertainment and Black Culture. It was going to be a star-studded show, to put it mildly.

Charles reinforced to me that I had to make sure everyone's tickets and passes were taken care of and none of the famous people would be held up at the door. No sooner than we had that conversation, the executives from Jet arrive to a mix up of them having no passes. Before Charles could get upset, the same thing happened to Jesse Jackson. Charles almost bit my head off. I rushed to the box office to handle the dilemma and was told by the box office manager that a Mr. Mark Green had come and taken all of the tickets and passes.

I yelled, "I am Mr. Mark Green!"

She responded that the Mark Green that came was tall and slim and wearing a gray suit. I contacted Bobby and Andre to help me resolve the situation. As we were talking, I noticed a young girl with a backstage pass on the upper left side of her chest. I needed to find out where she got the pass, because I was the only one issuing passes. I approached her and she said a guy had given her the backstage pass and luckily, he was walking past at the very moment, and she pointed him out. I approached him and as I was questioning him, he must've realized he had been busted and tried to break free from my hold. That's when Andre grabbed him by the neck and began to drag him in the back for a conference. That conference was more of a physical work out. We placed him against the wall and I checked his pockets. I opened his suit jacket and found several tickets and passes in his upper left-hand jacket pocket. I ripped his pocket out of his jacket and beat the shit out of him. I punched him in his face, stomach, and ribs. He fell to the ground and Andre and I began kicking him until he stopped responding to our beat down and then we picked him up and tossed him out the back door, just like in the movies.

I immediately grabbed the tickets and proceeded to the box office. After getting everyone situated, we found Bobby and told him about what had taken place. We laughed about it and began to prepare for the second show. Freddie was very popular in Chicago and we had two shows that night. As we got ready for the show, I noticed that the crook was "back in the building." He saw me and I proceeded to pursue him across the highway where he ran like he was running a marathon. He got the picture and never showed his face again.

When I got back to the hotel, I went to my room to count the money. I did not like the hotel because I was on the ground floor next to the parking lot and I had flashbacks of my college apartment where I was robbed. So, I made sure the room was secure, and my curtains were closed so no one could see inside.

I was piling my one-hundred grand on the bed in my usual stacks of denominations, when I was interrupted by the sound of the phone in my room. When I picked it up, I heard a voice asking me to verify that I was who I was, lived where I lived, and was born on the day that I was born. It was startling to hear my information rattled off to me like it was public information along with Bobby's and Andre's. He also said he was staying in the hotel and was going to kill me first then Bobby then Andre. I grabbed the money off the bed, threw it into my briefcase, and came up with a plan to make it out of there in one piece. I knew I had to get out of there fast!

I called security and requested an officer to escort us to another location, called Bobby and Andre to meet me at the front desk, and was out with whatever I could grab. My sense of relief at having an officer appear so quickly dissipated when he appeared with no gun or baton or back up. What kind of police officer doesn't have a gun?

It hit me that the crew had bought a few choice weapons at the Alamo, back in Texas. When we were there and everybody was making a fuss about getting a gun, I didn't see the urgency but now it was the greatest epiphany. I went into action. I called everyone who had copped a piece and told them to bring anything they had to me. In less than fifteen minutes, I had three pistols. My adrenaline was on a thousand. I gave one gun to Andre and kept the other two. I kept the .38 and the .44 and gave Andre the .357 Magnum.

One of the roadies, who was basically anonymous, said we could stay in his room as he was about to leave anyway. When we got to the room, the key wouldn't unlock the door and it was apparent that someone was on the other side of it. The officer knocked stating that he was an officer and the person yelled, "I don't care who you are, if you think you're coming in here you best believe you're gonna get shot!"

I was down the hall before he even completed his threat. He didn't have to warn me twice. All I could think of was that it was the same guy we had beaten up earlier who made the disturbing phone call. I ran into one of our truck drivers who had transported all of the equipment for the tour and he told me to get in the big rig. I climbed into the sleeper part of the truck and thought that the ordeal was over or at least that I could relax. Well, the thought was short-lived as I quickly realized I had another cocaine user with my life in his hands. Although he wasn't high on crack, the powder version of cocaine had him driving that truck like he was insane. He was so far gone, he must have been hallucinating and thinking he was driving a sports car.

Subsequently, I called the hotel to try to get to the bottom of how the assailant who had threatened me ended up two steps ahead and in one of the band mate's rooms. I mean, I really couldn't figure out how he knew what room we would show up to. It was much needed good news to find out that my "rescuer" had actually checked out, without letting us know at the time and the hotel had rented the room to another guest who must have felt just as confused as me when the police came knocking on his door. He didn't know anything about what was going on and obviously felt like he too was in danger and had to defend himself from us. What a relief!

## CHAPTER 17

# PIMPIN AIN'T EASY

Milwaukee, Wisconsin was the next place of business and a refuge. It was good to be alive and in the clear. When we walked into the lobby of the show, it looked like the "Player's Ball" with all the pimps, players, and drug dealers that the theater could hold. In talking to who I thought was a pimp after the show, I was educated on the difference between a "pimp" and a "mack" because although I thought he was a pimp, he told me he was not. A Pimp was in charge of paying his prostitutes but a Mack, like he claimed to be, gets taken care of by a woman.

Bobby and I began to know all of the drug dealers, pimps, macks, and players from state to state. Cocaine was becoming an epidemic and everyone from doctors to teachers to police officers were doing it. At one point, it was offered like a cigarette or a beer. Now people were cautious about who knew they did it and it became a running joke to me as I would say, **"There are those who do it and those who lie about doing it."** One of the problems I was having was dealing with the growing habits of some of the people who were on the road with us.

When we arrived in different cities, those who needed to find their "medicine" would travel to the hood to seek their "deliverance." They would find out where to get the drug of their choice and it would sometimes turn into a disaster as they would find themselves coming back late for rehearsal or late for the show and not always in their best state of mind. After binging, they were barely functioning.

On our travels to Minnesota, I decided to ride on one of the crew buses. There was a bodyguard by the name of King who was from South Central L.A. He looked like Barry White—big, Black, and full of processed curls on the top of his head. During a conversation, he paused to expose two grams of cocaine that he nonchalantly poured out onto the table between us. He proceeded to treat a few select people to a free sample of his product. When I asked him what his point was in doing that, he retorted, "Sit back and watch."

Moments later, they were open and spending money. It made sense. Who would pay for something they never tried and who wouldn't buy something that turned out to be good? The light bulb went off in my head after considering the fact that I was always with these people. Why should I make them have to wait until they went into unknown territory, when they were safe on the buses with me?

Surprisingly, Minnesota appeared to have a state full of Prince "look-alikes." Everyone had curly hair and was fair skinned. They all looked like they were bi-racial and that's probably because back when interracial dating and marriages were banned, Minnesota allowed the weddings to be held in that state.

Jimmy Jam and Terry Lewis were in attendance, and we met them and brought them backstage to meet Freddie. They welcomed us to their town and treated us like family. Freddie was hotter than fish grease and everyone wanted to meet him. Jimmy and Terry wanted to show us their town but we were in and out. However, the women in Minnesota all looked like models and stars. I think I fell in love about four times…lol.

## CHAPTER 18

# GOING BACK TO CALI

We were going to Cali for an appearance on the Joan Rivers show and I kept thinking about what King did on the bus and figured it would make sense to have a traveling "pharmaceutical dealer" with us so we could keep our people out of trouble and in our vicinity. That would alleviate them from going ghost on us.

Things were getting so bad with the drugs that I had to have two different hotel rooms. I had one to do my business and one room that was in a discreet location so I could rest. I needed a place where I wouldn't be interrupted at all hours of the night by people asking for advances on their money to go buy drugs. This wasn't your normal everyday life. This was life on the road in the music business so just like New York, the cities never sleep. There was always something going on and something for the crew to get into and that required funds and I was the one with the briefcase full of money. I could see if it was a simple exchange of money hand to hand, but this was still a business and the money had to be accounted for and I didn't feel like having to sign on the dotted line for an advance at three, four, or any random time of the morning, noon, or night. You gotta know that when someone is "feenin," they are nothing but uptight. They don't care what you're doing or what time it is. All they know is they need another hit. And I just wasn't havin' that shit. We had a light guy who lost his whole marriage over the fact that his twenty-five-hundred-dollar weekly salary would never make it home so eventually, he didn't have a home to go to. These are some of the sad stories and situations that I had to witness on a daily basis.

Life was bliss and I was enjoying every single bit of it. What people don't realize is after the movie *Scarface*, everyone wanted to be a dealer a hustler or a user. I compare it to the way weed is now—it's acceptable. That's how the drug scene was in the early 80s. You could not go to a party, show, or club without being around cocaine.

That's why I had to be very cautious about who I could and would let in my room. Although there were many times I wanted to be promiscuous, I didn't because the money was always with me, and there were a fair number of women who liked to set men up to be robbed. So, I had to be the serious one while everyone else had lots of fun.

One day, I ran into a female friend from my college years who had attended another school in the same area as mine. I invited her to go on the road with me for the weekend, to accompany me to one of our shows. She accepted my invitation and stayed with me for the weekend. I was a gentleman and let her sleep in her own bed. On the last night, however, I got a room with one king sized bed. I was excited that we would be sharing more than a room for the finale of the stay.

The evening was planned out perfectly. I had the room, the booze, and all the preparations were in place. I was finally going to be able to enjoy myself. As the conversation flowed and the wine kicked in, I could tell she was in a good mood and feeling intrigued by me and my lifestyle. As I began to make my move, there was a startling knock at the door. I acted like I heard nothing and moved forward for the kiss.

BOOM! BOOM! BOOM! BOOM! BOOM!

Just as I landed the kiss, she pushed me away and urged me to answer the door.

I yelled, "Who is it?!"

"It's me, Sonny. I need to get my money!"

"Sonny, I have company right now. Come back in an hour!"

He said, "No!" and started banging louder like there was a fire in the hallway.

He knocked louder and louder to the point where my guest demanded I go handle my business. I angrily got up and put on my shirt and proceeded to the door. I opened the door and started pleading with Sonny to just give me time, but he refused. We had several choice words and the next thing I knew, I was sucker punched in the face. Sonny was about 5'8 with glasses, a quiet type who looked like a librarian. I could not believe he'd sucker punched me, so I began to beat that ass like I was Mike Tyson. Before I knew it, Sonny ran off crying. I walked back into the room to find my date fully dressed with her luggage in hand.

"I want to leave. I don't want to be here anymore." Of course, that was the last thing I wanted to hear. I was begging and pleading when all of a sudden, there was another knock at the door. This time it was Al Goodman and Billy Brown from the group Ray Goodman and Brown. They asked me to come outside and discuss what had just happened. Sonny was standing there in tears. They could not believe the story because Sonny was so quiet and innocent and would not throw rice at a wedding let alone punch someone. I knew it was going to be a problem when they said they needed to speak to Charles Huggins.

As I went back to my room, my date was so angry she asked for her own room so I gave her mine and went to Andre's room to sleep on the couch. The next morning, I felt obligated to get her on a plane although I really wasn't feeling her reaction to what happened. We were quiet the whole ride to the airport and it was awkward. Although I was a little perturbed, I had to understand that the life I was living could be challenging for a woman who may be looking for something serious. I would think about her from time to time but the thoughts dissipated quickly because I never heard from her again.

As I usually did in retrospect, I was plotting my moves,

reflecting on how things could improve. My mind took me back to the idea of having an in-house supplier. I called JJ from Oakland who I had previously mentioned drove around in a Rolls. I offered him the opportunity to be "the man" but he turned it down. He offered up one of his boys, Mac, who was also from Oakland. Mac was interviewed and I hired him on the spot.

Mac was a conservative looking guy, tall and lanky with the appearance of an engineer. I liked that he didn't look flashy like his boy for obvious reasons. We flew Mac out and made the "crew" bus his home as he fit better there as opposed to the "band" bus. I must say for the record that in our particular circle, the band members were not messy nor did they indulge in illegal drugs. Kudos to them for never giving me any of the drama that came from some (not all) of the other groups and their crew members that traveled with us.

The deal was that Mac could only sell to the crew during their days off and only after the shows, on the day of a show. This turned out to work well. It gave the indulgers more focus as they knew they would be able to celebrate after completing their job responsibilities. So, it was a win-win for everyone! The shows ran smoother with less problems and of course, I received a portion of the sales.

The itinerary had us heading from Minnesota to Kansas, and then to Little Rock, Arkansas. The show in Kansas was scheduled for Easter Sunday but on Saturday, Mac informed me that he was sold out and had to "re-up." I panicked and he assured me that everything was going to be okay because he had a backup plan. I was relieved until I found out that the backup plan involved his mom. Of all the gangsters, hustlers, and shady people I had encountered, I had never done anything illegal with someone's mother.

He called his mother to ship him a package via an overnight delivery service. We went to the store and were a little tickled to see her creativity when we were handed a giant Easter bunny package with the works, including jelly beans and plastic eggs. It was definitely something a mom would send to her kid on Easter. It just didn't have what we were really looking for. We couldn't figure out where she had hidden the drugs and basically ripped everything apart looking for them. After calling his mom, she explained that she had cut the bunnies head off, stuffed the drugs inside the belly, and sewed it back up. Whew! We were relieved and very much impressed.

## CHAPTER 19

# JAMAICA FUNK

We left Kansas without any infractions. En route to Little Rock, Bobby and I began to talk about "Sweet Sweet Connie." There were groupies, and then there were "legendary tricks" and "Little Rock Connie" was one of them. She was a legend who had a song inspired by her and even in death, she was called Arkansas' most famous "Rock and Roll Groupie." Everyone had a "taste" or piece of Connie when they came to town, but the band "Grand Funk Railroad" went even further and put her in the lyrics to the song, "We're an American Band."

*Out on the road for forty days.*
*Last night in Little Rock put me in a haze.*
*Sweet Sweet Connie doing her act,*
*She had the whole show and that's a natural fact.*

The song was released in 1973 and went to number one and stayed on the Billboard charts for seventeen weeks. We were hoping to see what all the fuss was about and we actually got a chance to meet her when we got there. When the band was about to rehearse for the show, someone announced, "Little Rock Connie is here!" We were excited to see her and almost felt like a groupie to see

her in the flesh, because although we weren't interested in the "experience," just meeting her and being blessed with her beauty was enough. We could see why she was a legend in her time.

We were looking forward to being on the Joan Rivers show in the next two weeks but got a last-minute booking in Jamaica, so we flew out in between. Kingston, Jamaica was just as beautiful as you could imagine. The water, trees, and women were a nice break. Although we were there to work. working on an exotic island trumped some of the other destinations we had visited.

Upon arriving at the hotel, I met a young lady by the name of Shelly who I made friends with and who was our unofficial tour guide. She introduced me to a guy and divulged that I should have an escort who knew the land as it could be a dangerous situation for some tourists. My escort took me everywhere I wanted to go in town to handle my business and then it was time for me to experience the "hood" of Jamaica. I had never been to Jamaica before and knew nothing about their culture or customs. I was a little taken aback by the sights and wasn't interested in staying too long. The hotel, as in most foreign places, looked like paradise, while the actual citizens were living in poverty.

When I reached the luxurious resort where we were staying, my boss, Kevin Harewood, decided to take me to enjoy some authentic Jamaican cuisine. We came upon a local "chef" who was cooking chicken on the side of the road, which is fine and not alarming however, he was cooking the chicken inside of a hub cap. That wasn't my idea of trying a fancy delicacy. Kevin informed me that that was how it" was done.

When I looked at the plate, it looked so good that I had to psych myself out and forget I had just seen it in something that would be on the outside of a car tire which rides on dirty roads. I had to push past my apprehension and tell myself that it probably wouldn't instantly kill me. Man was I surprised when it tasted like the best chicken I had ever had! When I inquired as to what the dish was called, I was told I had just devoured "jerk chicken." This began a lifetime love affair with me and jerk chicken. Even all of these years later, I have it at least once a week.

After the show, Shelly and I went out for drinks. She was a native of Kingston and shared some of her life experiences with me. We exchanged numbers and vowed to keep in touch. Little did I know that years later, I would be hearing from her with the admission that she had moved to Florida. That's nice, I thought. But what did that have to do with me?

We talked for awhile and I told her to reach back out if she was ever in New York. A year later, I got another call in which she informed me that she had not only moved to New York but was very close to where I was in Long Island. I contemplated on whether to go out with her or not, not knowing if she had any ulterior motives. I decided to go out with her, and we had a great time. We dated for a short while and she remains a very close friend to this day.

After Kingston, we had a show in Montego Bay. Everything turned out great and I fell in love with Jamaica. It turned out to be my once-a-year visit for more than ten years. After Jamaica, we flew back to Los Angeles, where we had a few days off before the Joan Rivers Show. For me, L.A. was exciting. It was much different than N.Y.C. because of its bright lights, fast cars, and movie stars. I was in heaven.

My first encounter with Joan Rivers was a memorable and motivating one because she was making a name for herself as a talk show host having been a stand-up comedienne for many years. She was just as funny as you would expect. Meeting her husband, Edgar Rosenberg, was monumental as well because he was a powerhouse in television. When you find yourself in rooms and hobnobbing with people known for their fame and fortune, it really feels good and like you have arrived. (Although "arriving" can be a constant thing).

Thirty years later, I encountered Joan Rivers again, at Bergen PAC where I booked her for a show. That time, she not only remembered me from coming on her show so many years before but felt comfortable enough to call me on my cell phone and ask me if I was "ready to have her for dinner." I felt like Eddie Murphy in Boomerang with Eartha Kitt. I figured she was just joking because that was her sense of humor. Either way, she was a joy to hang out with.

## CHAPTER 20

# HOUSE OF PAIN

We flew from L.A. to D.C, one of Freddie's hottest markets. He had sold out two shows there and it was the last city of the tour, so everyone was excited. My college friend, Red, had plans to throw a party for me, upon my arrival back into town.

Red and I shared an apartment one summer during college. He was very ambitious and always desired the finer things in life. He had champagne taste and beer money. But after he left school, he got into sales and began to do well for himself. He had the gift of gab and could sell you an ocean view apartment in the desert. He also had a way with women. He always had a dime piece on his arm and one on the side. He was very excited to host me in D.C. and I was happy to see him.

As I arrived in D.C., Charles reminded me, as always, that he would be stopping through to collect the proceeds from the tour the next day. He said to expect him to be at my hotel room around 9 a.m. Due to the amount of money, I always kept it with me because I didn't trust the hotels or the housekeepers. But this time, I decided to leave it in the security box, in the hotel lobby. I don't know what made me change my usual routine, except that sometimes you just have a gut feeling or as they say, "follow your first thought," but I was glad I did. *(Rule #10: Trust Your Gut and Not Your Feelings)*

After the show, Red was excited for me to come to the party, although I really didn't feel up to it. I was shocked to see that there was a whole setup with a smorgasbord of food stations, carving stations, and unlimited drinks flowing. I felt like "The man" I was.

There was a DJ playing all the hits of that year. The place was grand just like the setup and although it looked like it could hold about a thousand or more people, I guess they all didn't get their invitations because there were only about seven people in attendance. I was flattered by his gesture, but not impressed by the turn out. We took the "group" to his hotel room for the after party. He had a two-bedroom suite to play in with the five of us guys and two females that followed.

I agreed to go with everybody but when the party started, I immediately saw the type of party it truly was going to be. Red dumped an ounce of cocaine on the table and that's when I knew it was time for me to go. I was done with that scene and had my mind on my money and my money on my mind. It was already about two or three in the morning and I had had several drinks and smoked some weed, which just made me want to do nothing but crash in my hotel bed. I was in one of the rooms in the suite and was preparing to make my exit. A young lady popped in. She was high and wanted some attention. She began talking and would not shut up. I, on the other hand, dozed off as the conversation turned one sided.

All I remember is waking up the next morning in the same room. I obviously had passed out, so I knew I had to get back to my room to meet with Charles. I checked my watch to see what time it was and realized that my wrist was bare. My watch was gone. I patted myself down and my money and jewelry were gone too. I was in shock. How did this happen? I yelled out to Red, but he was busy, I guess entertaining or passed out too, in the other suite. I didn't have time to wake him up, I had to rush out to meet Charles. I called Bobby and he asked, "Where the hell you been? Charles has been calling and banging on your door. He's very angry."

When I entered my room, I was greeted by a piece of paper on the floor, which had been put under my door. "You're fired and drop the money off to Andre." I was devastated to think that my dream job would be a thing of the past. I couldn't believe it and boy was I mad at Red.

Red didn't even understand the magnitude of what he had caused. He wasn't a hard-working individual like me who had gotten where I did through blood, sweat, and tears. He was a hustler. He didn't value nor desire hard work. He drove a red Maserati and lived the fast life. Money came easy and when it went, he knew how to get it again. That was not my path. I loved my career in entertainment and nothing was worth losing it over. I didn't know what to do and foolishly let Red convince me to move down to D.C. At that point, I had no other option. Red agreed to pay me a salary because he wanted me to break him in the industry. He had plenty of money he had acquired through real estate and flipping powder.

People thought Red was a drug dealer, but he was just in it for the fun and had no intention of trying to be the next Scarface. He just enjoyed the attention it brought to him.

Red was wining and dining me to persuade me to stay in D.C. and help him open a nightclub. He "practiced" his profession by going to all of the expensive restaurants that he could find and ordering bottle service and "flossing like he was a Boss."

After weeks of looking, he found a location for the club. It was an old warehouse that was close to a residential area. Before I could blink an eye, he had the construction workers in there day and night trying to prepare for the grand opening. In the meantime, I was selling club memberships and collecting money. As we got closer and closer, the idea of the club began to be a reality. I remember walking into the club and all the structures were up, including the bathrooms and the VIP area. However, I knew there was no way we would have the club up and running by New Year's Eve but I kept on selling membership and enjoying the lifestyle in D.C.

Red's club was supposed to open on New Year's Eve, but my boy did not do all of the homework to get it open. He neglected to make sure the location was zoned for that type of venue. It wasn't. Money spent. Money lost. No biggie to Red. I could not believe he put so much money in the club and did not meet the zoning requirements. Let alone all the money we collected from people and not to mention that we spent it all on good times. At times, he was too trusting and parting way too much to make sound decisions.

That was just one occasion where Red exhibited poor business practices. Red was so caught up in his own hype that he started getting sloppy and messing with the wrong people. One of the guys he thought was his flunky did a number on him. I saw it coming, clear as day. Red liked the power that his image brought him and thought his "workers" were loyal. **Rule # 5 (C.R.E.A.M.)** I tried to warn him about one guy but he felt he had him under control. The guy just rubbed me the wrong way but I couldn't tell Red that because he knew what he was doing. Or so he thought. I picked up the guy's vibe and it was bad. Red liked to order him around and one day he placed an "order" for some product and sent the guy to retrieve it. Well, he did follow orders to pick up the package. The only problem was that he never returned with it. He made off with Red's product and a rental car that Red was using. Unfortunately, we never heard from that guy ever again.

There was another friend of Red's who was a hustler that we used to hang out with from time to time. I happened to like the guy. We would go out on the town and bounce back and forth to clubs. Spending crazy money on unnecessary things like jewelry, expensive champagne, and women. Or just sit around and party 'til we all passed out. When out of nowhere, Red received a phone call that the guy had been shot and killed. That was my signal to exit stage NORTH. It was time to head back to NYC and away from the D.C. madness. I was getting too comfortable with this free style of living and surrounding myself with low lives. I needed to get my game back and focus on my career. So, I packed my stuff and bounced back to New York.

One good thing that happened years later involved Red showing up to my house for a party. With him was the girl who'd robbed me. As soon as I saw her, I went loco on her to the point that Red made her take off all her jewelry, including a rope chain with a gold medallion, and give it to me. Then he sent her back home on the train the same night. Years later I ran into her in D.C., and she asked for her jewelry back. I looked at her and laughed.

## CHAPTER 21

# TOO LEGIT TO QUIT

As fate would have it, I received a call from Louise West, a high-powered entertainment lawyer. She wanted me to be the road manager for her artist, Glenn Jones. His hits were "Here We go Again," "Show Me," and "We've Only Just Begun." I had built a name for myself as a road manager and tour manager so I couldn't wait to get back in the game and on the road again doing what I do best!

Going on the road with Glenn was enjoyable because he was a humble and low-key artist. He was one of my most drama free performers. I worked with Glenn for about three months and it was cool and easy. But the real gem of the partnership was getting to be around Louise because she had the insight on the business and where it was going. She had many of the up-and-coming groups, and I was interested in working with her further. I had dreams of opening my own business and knew she would be an asset to that endeavor, even if just by giving great advice. I really did not know much about her but word on the street was she was the person you need to know if you want to gain knowledge and be successful.

As I was finishing the tour with Glenn, I got a call from Andre Harrell. He was running Uptown Records and had an entourage of groups on the label that I was definitely interested in working with. I had met Andre on the road when he had his own rap group, Dr. Jekyll and Mr. Hyde. We had already had somewhat of a relationship, but as the head of Uptown, he wanted to pair me up with his new artist Al B. Sure. The ladies loved Al B. Sure and I jumped at the chance to capitalize on his success. Al was about six feet tall and light-skinned with curly hair. He was every girl's dream of a light-skinned pretty boy.

I'll never forget being on the road with him. Al was selling out places left and right. He was definitely one that would reach super star status. I remember walking into RFK Stadium and almost getting hit in the face with the shower of panties that women were throwing at him. I had never experienced anything like it. The screams, the crying, and the falling out. In the back of my mind I was like, who is this guy!?

As we were exiting the stadium, a young lady by the name of April Harris approached me with her demo. I took her info and never listened to the demo and passed it on to my friend George Harrell (no relation to Andre). At the time, I was mentoring George and showing him the ropes. I had already told Andre that I was not going to be on the road long because I had other career desires. Given that, he asked me to train George and prepare him for the handoff.

Years later, April became a star and was the founding member of the group, Seduction, with their main hit

"Heartbeat." I was not surprised because I had made that mistake several times while on the road. Over and over again.

Another guy who approached me about being a singer was a guy named Stevie who I met in Miami. He was a promoter booking rap concerts in 1985 when we met. He talked about being a singer but it was not enough to make me listen. He later became a dancehall star by the name of "Stevie B" who ruled the dance scene for more than a decade.

As the Al B. Sure tour continued, we picked up a comedian who was another star in the making. No one knew him at the time. He wasn't big or even that noticeable. He was just someone to open the show up and we had seen many show openers come and go but not this one. We didn't know him then, but we all know him now. His name is Chris Rock.

I don't remember a lot about Chris other than him being a comedian and just an opener at the time. Al was the main focus and he was hotter than a stolen car trying to cross the border.

AL B. SURE! US TOUR 1988

| JULY | | | | PAGE |
|---|---|---|---|---|
| TUE | 5 | SPRINGFIELD, MA | DAY OFF | 1 |
| WED | 6 | SPRINGFIELD, MA | MARRIOTT HOTEL | 2 |
| THU | 7 | POUGHKEEPSIE, NY | THE CHANCE | 3 |
| FRI | 8 | SYRACUSE, NY | GARDENIAS | 4 |
| SAT | 9 | RICHMOND, VA | MARRIOTT HOTEL | 5 |
| SUN | 10 | WASHINGTON, DC | RFK STADIUM | 6 |
| MON | 11 | NEW HAVEN, CT | DAY OFF | 7 |
| TUE | 12 | NEW HAVEN, CT | TOAD'S PLACE | 8 |
| WED | 13 | SAG HARBOR, NY | BAY STREET | 9 |
| THU | 14 | ALBANY, NY | EMPIRE STATE PLAZA | 10 |
| FRI | 15 | STANFORD, CT | WESTIN HOTEL | 11 |
| SAT | 16 | PROVIDENCE, RI | THE RHODES | 12 |
| SUN | 17 | SAYERVILLE, NJ | CLUB BENE | 13 |
| MON | 18 | ATLANTIC CITY, NJ | HARRAH'S | 14 |
| TUE | 19 | ATLANTIC CITY, NJ | DAY OFF | 15 |
| WED | 20 | HARRISBURG, PA | METRON | 16 |
| THU | 21 | MONROEVILLE, PA | TOP CHARLIES | 17 |
| FRI | 22 | COLUMBUS, OH | NEWPORT MUSIC CENTER | 18 |
| SAT | 23 | FT. WAYNE, IN | EMBASSY THEATRE | 19 |
| SUN | 24 | CINCINNATI, OH | BOGARTS | 20 |
| MON | 25 | INDIANAPOLIS, IN | DAY OFF | 21 |
| TUE | 26 | INDIANAPOLIS, IN | PICCADILLY | 22 |
| WED | 27 | CHARLOTTE, NC | DAY OFF | 23 |
| THU | 28 | CHARLOTTE, NC | DAY OFF | 24 |
| FRI | 29 | CHARLOTTE, NC | COLISEUM | 25 |
| SAT | 30 | ATLANTA, GA | FULTON CO. STADIUM | 26 |

Halfway through the tour, I decided to focus on my new direction. I wanted to be a record executive, so I told Andre I was ready to bounce. George, on the other hand, was from Harlem and was very hungry to get into the business as well. I was living in Hempstead, Long Island and George would take the train every day to come and sit with me and take notes and direction. I liked George because he was determined and had the street knowledge needed to do the job. When I felt that George was ready, I informed Andre, and passed the baton.

Although I had planned to leave, Andre tried to get me back by offering me another tour. This time it was with the rap artist, Heavy D. It was inviting but I had to stick to my guns and stay focused on my personal goal. I did him the favor and sat down and met with Heavy but I showed him no interest. I wanted into the record business.

## CHAPTER 22

# MIDNIGHT HOUR

I had not forgotten about my passion for music production. I called my longtime college friend, Krush, and asked if he wanted to start a production team and a record label. Krush was a DJ too. He was from Hollis, Queens and we had similar tastes. I had pledged Krush when we were in college and took a liking to him.

We began talking about setting up our label and producing and writing. The first line of business was to come up with a name for our label. I came up with "On Que" because we were both brothers from the Omega Psi Phi fraternity and pulling up a track was called queuing up a record. I thought the name was catchy and it identified who we were and what we did.

*DJ Krush*

Krush added some other members of his crew to join the team. Kevin Presley, a bass player, and Eric Sutton, another DJ. The crew was called the "SGL Productions."

We talked about making a record about Hip-Hop and how it was still not mainstream. Most Hip-Hop tracks were only played after midnight at the time, so the song was going to be based on the Wilson Pickett song, "Midnight Hour."

Krush brought a girl from Queens to the studio. She looked young and innocent. She did not look hardcore like most female rappers of that time. But she had mad skills. After we helped her write the first song, we were on and poppin! Our creative flow was like no other. We all made contributions to each song. It was a marriage made in heaven.

During that same time, I saw an ad in the trades for a marketing rep at a distribution company by the name CEMA which stood for Capital Emi Manhattan and Angel Records. The company was in Hackensack, the same town I was living in. I just knew the job was meant for me.

I applied for the job and landed it. My boss called me that evening to invite me to a business dinner for me to meet everyone at the company. He was nice enough to pick me up and let me ride with him, which is not customary in most companies. He was also nice enough to offer me a joint that he lit as soon as I got in the car. I took it as a courtesy. I didn't want to turn it down, because it was almost as offensive as not eating at someone's home when they offer you food. I made a statement without saying anything, by only taking one pull. I wanted him to know up front that I wasn't there to party. He got the message.

As time went on, I was a bit secluded because I wasn't partaking in the festivities that regularly took place. Every Friday certain individuals that were part of the clique, stayed behind to enjoy some libations and fun. Until the fateful day that a co-worker asked me if I knew where to get some coke. I said yes and provided him with the product. I went from the loner to "that guy." Unfortunately, every Friday my boss wanted me to make a "run" for him.

Every Friday was a real-life rendition of the song, "Just got Paid, it's Friday Night." They partied every week and it became a burden for me. While they safely awaited my return, I was out there risking my freedom for them. It wasn't worth it. At first, I thought it was cool. That I was now part of the crew and got mad respect. However, as I began to analyze my situation, I started to feel like I was being used.

One night around midnight, my boss called and asked me to go to Harlem and I told him I couldn't do it because I had to work in the morning. I thought that might work but he answered, "I'm your boss!" I explained the amount of time it would take me to get from Westwood, NJ, where I was living at the time, to Hackensack, NJ to get the money, then to Harlem, and back. It would have been a three-hour tour.

He was understanding and gave a solution that sounded like it made sense at the time. He wanted the location of the coke spot so he could go on his own. I gave him the information and no sooner than they arrived at the destination, were they pulled over by the police. Two white guys in a car with New Jersey license plates entering a known drug zone at 1 a.m. He told me his "co-defendant" shitted on himself when the cops turned on their sirens and pulled over the car. Eventually they were let go. We laughed about it over the years, but I was glad it was over. What was great was that the ordeal set me free from the obligation. He found someone else who would make deliveries and I found relief.

As a marketing rep at the company, I was dealing with product placement in stores, marketing artists, creating avenues for promotions and basically manipulating the retail reps for airplay. During one of our dinner meetings with one of the big wigs that I was seated next to, I was asked a bunch of questions about Black music and the culture of the music industry in general. It started out as a general conversation, but I noticed after a while that he was solely focused on me and my knowledge of that side of the business. I didn't know who he was or why he was picking my brain, but it was my area of passion and expertise, so it was natural for me to discuss those things with people.

At the end of the dinner, he gave me his card and told me to keep in touch. I was astonished to see that this dude was the President of Chrysalis Records Worldwide. He wasn't "Mr. Biggs" but "Mr. Big Big!"

The next day my boss asked if I knew who I was sitting next to the night before and when he shared who he was, he also shared that he wanted to hire me to head the R&B department of Chrysalis Records in New York. I was excited but that was short-lived when my boss explained that he had told the guy that I wasn't ready for such a position. I was angry and asked him why he stopped that enormous blessing for me and he nonchalantly said, "I didn't want to have to find another Black guy and if I did find one, he wouldn't know the wealth of things you do. Everybody loves you here anyway." He almost shrugged his shoulders and said it matter-of-factly. I was furious on the inside. I never forgot that and continued to work with Krush and my own company in the studio, while planning my exit.

We finished our first draft of the record, and I was so excited to bring it to Kool DJ Red Alert to have it played on the air. Red Alert was the biggest DJ in Hip-Hop. He ruled the airwaves for more than two decades. His only real competition was Chuck Chillout and his side kick Funkmaster Flex. Red and I formed a friendship while we were on the Fresh Fest in 1985, he was the DJ for Sparky D and I was the road manager for the Boogie Boys. We both came up from the Hip-Hop game and had mad respect for each other. Red listened to the demo and dropped the bomb on me that in his words, "You ain't there yet." So back to the studio we went.

In the meantime, there was another group recording at the studio while we were there, and we would always run into them. We would see them as we were leaving. However, we never had any real conversation other than "What's up." In my mind, they were our competition. They were called, "The New Style."

*Glynice Coleman, Varnell Johnson &*
*Mark Green*

Their record "OPP" was what they were working on and when they dropped that record, they changed the group name to the now famous "Naughty by Nature."

Back at CEMA, I was getting antsy because I wanted to be promoted. After what happened to me by missing that great opportunity, I knew I had no real future there and I needed to keep it moving! My break was right around the corner. Shortly thereafter, a lady named Glynice Coleman came to offer me a position at EMI Records. I was psyched. We had work together at CEMA and she told me she liked my work and wanted to bring me on. She took me to meet Varnell Johnson, the VP of Promotions. I sat down with Varnell and I remembered him when I was on tour with Freddie Jackson. Not knowing who he was at the time, I gave him a hard time when he tried to get backstage to see Freddie. However, he did not remember me and I never brought the situation up. We talked and I could tell VJ was from the streets and knew his shit. They decided to give me a job and immediately made me head of Retail Sales and Jazz Promotions.

## CHAPTER 23

# MUSIC IS THE MESSAGE

I wasn't that happy about my title but figured I would get in the company first and then see where I could go from there. Within months we signed our first rap record. It was by Jaz and Jay-Z called, "Hawaiian Sophie." The record was a corny bubblegum type record. I didn't see it as a hit, but someone did.

There was a white guy heading the Rap division and it wasn't his color that was the problem, he was just a fish out of water. He had no knowledge of rap music. That was the division for me, not him. I challenged him in a staff meeting in front of all the executives. It was my only chance to show them who was really the right man for that job. I ran circles around him in the meeting and thought I was "In like Flynn," but not so fast.

I was telling the executives that our rap department was garbage and making not only this guy look incompetent, but I was also unknowingly offending the executives who had signed the artists because they were the ones who greenlit the projects, not him. While I thought I was painting a good picture of myself, I was digging my own grave.

It didn't dawn on me until after the meeting when people came up to me and asked me if I "saw the vice president's face when you were 'trashing his name' verbally." In my mind I thought, "Oh shit."

Let's just say, he didn't care much for me after that, but I still had my job and my goal to "go all the way up" wasn't deterred. At the time, all I wanted to do was run the rap department and blow it up. As time went on, I found a demo from a guy in Virginia. As soon as I heard his record, I knew it was a hit. I shopped it to Capitol Records and

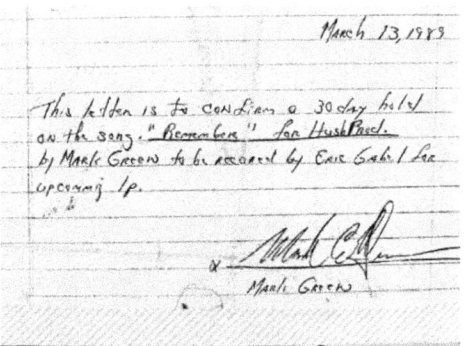

as many other labels as I could. The time came when I had to humble myself. I had to go and ask the same vice president to sign this artist. You can imagine what he said, right? NO.

I took the demo to Uptown Records, but I did not intend to use the artist, just sell the song to another performer. Kurt Woodley, the head of A&R loved the song and it was intended for Jeff Redd, but somehow it never happened. So, I then took it to my old company, Hush Productions. They loved the song and gave me their word that I would be able to produce the record. Unfortunately, they hired another producer and gave the record to a new singer by the name of Eric Gable.

The record began to climb the charts and although I

wasn't the producer, I had publishing on the record. The name of the record was "Remember the First Time" on EMI Records and it became number one on the R&B charts in 1990.

After about a year, I realized I hadn't collected any royalties. I immediately called my Power of Attorney, Louise West, and she met with me to break the business down to me. She explained the publishing "game" and gave the steps to starting my own business. She reached out to Capitol Records and was able to get them to send me all of the funds that were owed to me.

After delivering the record to EMI, I was promoted to Director of Urban Marketing and I reported to the Pop department. I was proud of myself and ready to grab this new bull by the horns.

I was still handling the new Rap department and Jaz and Jay-Z were the newbies we were developing. I went out on the road a couple of times with the pair, but it turned out that the label was having a lot of pushback from Jaz. They weren't feeling him and weren't interested in moving forward with him on the next project. To them, he was very difficult to work with and no one wanted the job of babysitting him.

On one occasion, when I was alone with Jay-Z, he played a record for me titled, "The Originator." I was in shock and knew another hit was coming down the pike that I would get to be a part of and I would also get to watch another star be born. I was like a kid in a candy store. What was cool about Jay-Z was that he was humble and quiet. He was basically there to support Jaz as a DJ but had serious lyrical skills. From that point on, I hung onto Jay-Z like loose change.

One day when they came to the office, they had their bodyguard, Harry Fobbs, with them. Harry would put you in the mind of Biggie. Harry was a historian of Hip-Hop music, knowing every song and lyric that you could think of. He was about 6'3 and never smiled. He had a big scar on the left side of his face that made him look like Scarface. Glynice Coleman took a liking to Harry and gave him a position as the manager of the Rap department. I was happy for him because he

*Harry Fobbs & Mark Green*

was a talented dude, and he deserved the break. I had a whole lot going on and was glad he would take the baton as I passed it.

Harry and I would spend every day together going to lunch and talking about the business. I schooled him on everything I knew because Harry was from the streets and did not understand the corporate way of doing business. That did not stop him as he was determined to make a name for himself and he was on his way. Just as Harry started to make real money and move up the corporate ladder, his life changed overnight.

One night, while in Washington D.C. on our way out on the town, Harry fell to the ground and I was totally freaked out. He yelled out my name for help and I ran over to him to try and get him up. With Harry being 6'3 and about 300 pounds, I had a very hard time getting him up. As soon as I did, I helped him limp back to the hotel where I called for an ambulance. They rushed him to the hospital where he was later sent to NYC. Harry was in a lot of pain and seeing him cry—a guy who never smiled and who looked like he'd killed several people—was hard for me to watch. Harry would go on to stay in the hospital for months where he later passed. His death was very hard for me because we had become so close. It took me a long time to get back to normal and I would often think about his journey and his accomplishments.

As time would have it, I was still working on my Hip-Hop record and took the advice of Red Alert and decided to make some changes. I came up with the idea to add Latin keys to the record. It was a familiar Latin rift that everyone knew. No one before me had mixed Latin music with Hip-Hop.

I didn't wait to go back to Kool DJ Red Alert. This time I just pressed up the record and dropped it off at Kiss FM. About a week later, I was driving down the street when I couldn't believe my ears. My record came on. I was so happy and shocked that I rolled down all the windows and blasted it loudly. I could not believe my song was on the radio! Within another two weeks, I heard the b side on the dance station. We had use MSFB 'Music is the message" and sampled it with rap lyrics underneath the track. Bam! Another hit!

The next day I went back to the record label hoping they would sign the record. I had to face the Vice President of A & R again. He had the keys in his hand, so I had to suck it up. Again, he denied me.

The record was getting a lot of airplay so I wasn't going to stop there. I came up with another idea. Instead of me going to keep asking, I decided to send Krush to get the job done. Krush looked straight out of a Hip-Hop catalog. He had all the gear and the look but he had no knowledge of how the business worked so I had to prep him before he went in. I told him what to say and do. By the time he was done talking, they wanted to sign the record and hire him at the label. I tried to convince him to take the job but Krush didn't feel competent enough to handle the position as again, he had no experience. He stated that he had only done what I told him to do.

After we got the deal, we received a $10,000 check for the single. Videos at that time were that price and I felt it was a good investment to show EMI that we were serious about our product and were going to push it and not just wait around for them to do so. I went to NYU Film school and asked for the best film student and found a director to shoot our video for $5,000. Ironically, the kid, Chris, grew up a few blocks from me and he was the little brother of my close friend Freddie Williams.

We shot the video and played it for the EMI staff but they weren't that impressed with it. That was about the last stop that the video took because they didn't release it, shop it, or promote it.

The record, on the other hand, ironically started taking on a life of its own. It traveled to Texas, Boston, and other states without the partnership of the video. The video did not stop the show, just like one monkey can't. There was an article written about the girl that rapped on "Midnight Hour" that was titled, "Lady Spice Raps Kinda Nice!" I was

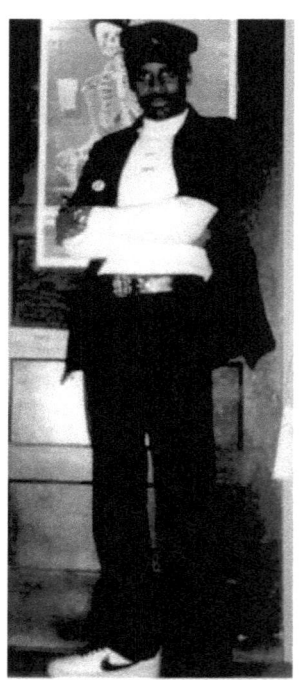

*DJ Krush*

glad to see my hard work starting to be recognized.

## CHAPTER 24

# MORE MONEY MORE PROBLEMS

They say more money, more problems, but I didn't have a lot of money. But I started having people think I did, which caused problems. I spent half of the money on the video and some of my coworkers in the promotions department wanted a kick back and threatened not to work my project if I didn't give it to them.

After about a month, the record flatlined. EMI was not clear on how to market or promote this new genre of music, Rap, and the end came not long after the beginning. The record was short lived to put it mildly.

We didn't stop there. We had another project lined up. A guy from Brooklyn, named Johnnie Wah, who went to college with us, had shown promise as a Hip-Hop artist and we put some energy towards his career because he was a true performer. He had all the skills needed to entertain—charisma, talent, and swag. He was a true storyteller, like Biggie. His delivery was clear and animated. After recording a few demos, we landed a deal with the late Joey Robinson, Jr. He had a label under MCA records, Bona Ami records.

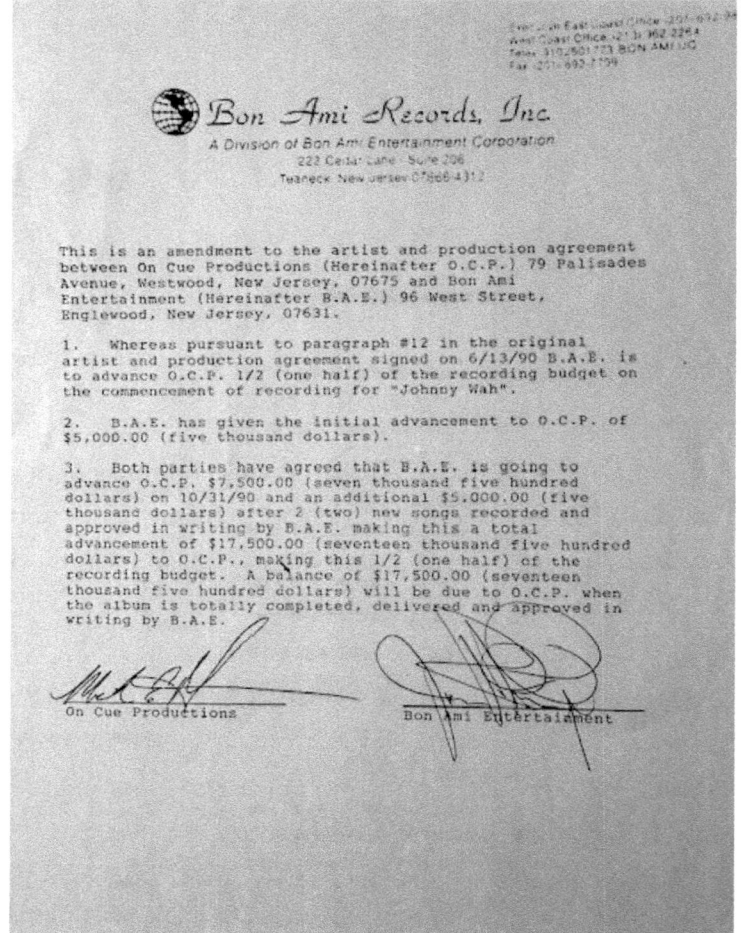

We were all excited about the deal. The contract was $40,000 but we only received $7,000 the day we had the meeting to sign it. This was an immediate red flag as this was not what we had agreed to contractually. We continued to work on the album, but the album never actually came out. The worst part of it was that we were bound to the label by the contract and could not go anywhere else and could not get our $33,000 from the guy.

I tried with several attorneys, but everyone was scared of Mr. Robinson and the ties he had to the music business, so we never received the rest of our money. But as always, *the show must go on!*

As in other disappointing times, we never skipped a beat. We went back in the studio to work with another artist named Fonda Rae. Fonda was known in the dance world. She had a big crossover record call "Over Like A Fat Rat" and a couple other known records. This time we incorporated two singers from Virginia State University, Barry Wells and Tony McGriff. Because they had sung together for many years, their harmony was like no other at that time. They reminded me of Mc Fadden and Whitehead. I imagined them doing justice to a song that used to be my favorite, "I heard it through the grapevine" by Gladys Knight and the Pips. We recorded the remake and a rap track to it and made it current to the times.

The two guys and Fonda Rae brought that song back and current. I was pleased with it but we couldn't get a deal on the song. I was bummed out. It wasn't until recently that I found out the song had actually done some good numbers overseas from a guy I used to press up the records. He took our master and sold it overseas. As I learned in this business, you can't trust anyone. *(Rule #1: Trust No One)*

Out of nowhere, Darryl decided to call it quits after that, putting the nail in the coffin of our production team. We had been given some recognition, but we just didn't get that hit that would make us "Too Legit to Quit" like MC Hammer.

The song says it's hard to say goodbye to yesterday, but it was my future that I felt like I was saying goodbye to. When the dust settled, I bounced back because I never left. I still had my job at EMI Records. I was the Director of the Urban Marketing department, yet I reported to the Pop department. Working in these two different departments was as different as night and day. As much as I loved working in Marketing, I really wanted to be in the Urban department working with my peers. It was weird though. When I was working with the Urban department, I was treated like an outsider and when I was in the Pop department, I was treated like a King. We're talking about town cars vs. limousines or motels vs. 5-star luxury hotels.

**Mark Green Upped To New EMI Post**

Phil Blume, National Director, Sales, EMI Records, has announced the promotion of Mark "Money" Green to the position of National Urban Marketing Manager, a newly created post. In his new position, Green, based in New York, will be involved with all the aspects of selling and marketing the label's Urban product.

**Mark Green**

Said Blume in making the announcement: "The creation of this position and Mark's promotion into it is further testimony to EMI's continued commitment to the ongoing success of our Black music. Money's knowledge and understanding of not just the Urban music scene, but the music industry in general, as well as his determination and loyalty to this label, have earned him the important new position here."

Even still, I wanted to work in Urban. Soon thereafter, we got a new President at the label and they shook everything up and it was like an old five and dime store when they would close and put a sign in the window that reads, "Everything Must Go!" My boss and all of the other vice presidents were fired, and they had to be replaced.

I couldn't believe they'd fired Varnell Johnson. He had done so much for the company and brought so many streams of revenue. I can't say I sulked too long because the rainbow came after the rain.

Glynice Coleman! My mentor. My confidante. My coach and the one who groomed me for this job, was now the vice president of the Urban department! She reached out to me and asked me to join her and it was something I had always wanted.

I wish I knew then what I know now because it wasn't a good move. It was actually one of the worst moves I had ever made in my career.

I realized very early that being in promotions just didn't have as much of an opportunity for growth nor did I have the diversity I had in marketing. Nevertheless, I did my job the way I was supposed to without slacking. One thing I always was, is a person of my word. So, I took the job and was dedicated to it.

After receiving my promotions job, I did what any professional would do—seek out the gurus of the game. That's when I looked for Thelma and Louise, Laverne and Shirley, Cagney and Lacey AKA Jodi Williams and Hilda Williams. These two ladies had the promotion game on lock and I would spend days and nights hanging with them and gaining knowledge.

Jodi Williams had so much game that if she was a man, she would have been a pimp. Hilda was the smooth operator who could sell water to a well. That's how business savvy and creative she was. Being around them helped me to continue to elevate my game, and my craft.

EMI Records signed Smokey Robinson and his first single was a frisbee and bombed like no one would ever imagine. The staff was responsible for breaking the record on the radio. I covered the tri-state area and Smokey had a show in Atlantic City and I had to convince the Program Director of a popular radio station to come to see the show. He agreed with stipulations. He needed:

1. Weed
2. Two bottles of Dom Perignon
3. A dozen roses for his date
4. An expensive suite at a very expensive hotel

When I arrived at the show, I immediately ran into Smokey's dressing room where he was getting ready for the show. The first thing Smokey asked was where's the Programming Director. I had to lie to him and tell him that the guy was on his way and said he would stop by and see him after the show. I called his phone over and over again but not enough to make him pick it up. He never answered any of my calls. I sat there the whole night agonizing over all the funds that were wasted to get this guy to show, for him to be a no-show.

Back in the office some days later, I went into the team meeting and couldn't think of a story that was good enough to fabricate the real one. I had no approach and no desire to be honest but I had to be in attendance. Fortunately, I came out of the meeting victorious and on top of my game! I was informed that I was the only one on the staff that got the record added on the radio. Although the Program Director had let me down at first, he came through when it mattered most.

CHAPTER 25

# SOMEBODY'S WATCHING ME

Things began to pick up quickly. I was given another territory, the mid-Atlantic, to cover radio. My good friend Chico and I were both handling two regions at a time as local regional reps. We spent a lot of time together flying back and forth from Washington, D.C. and Virginia. When we were not flying, we were driving back and forth from Philly. Another friend who collaborated with us was Penny Chan. Penny and I had a great friendship and spent time motivating each other. Whenever Chico and I were not in the air, Penny and I were driving to the next station.

On one occasion after returning from the road, I was brought into a room with the A&R Director, the VP of Promotions, and the VP of EMI. I guess he wanted me to witness what he was about to say. The VP of EMI went right in on the director of A&R.

"I can't believe you passed on Mariah Carey, Vanilla Ice, and Brian McKnight! You don't have a Black bone in your body!" he said scolding the A&R Director.

"Look at the talent you passed on!" It was true, a deaf man could hear that talent. I would have signed Vanilla Ice just because he was a white version of MC Hammer who already had a major success story. With no more conversation, he fired the Director of A&R.

Things got really ugly before they got good again. It just so happened that year that EMI made so much money they gave all the executives twenty percent bonuses of their salaries. I made a $20,000 bonus and I used the money as a down payment on my first house. I truly owe my decision to my father. I had no intention on buying a house. I was too happy flying around spending money on tailormade suits, alligator shoes and jewelry. Then one day, my father asked me how much I made and then he told me I need to buy a house. I agreed but kept doing my thing. There was a house on the block where we lived and an elderly couple was trying to sell it so they could return back to the South. My father had me look at the house. It was garbage to me and I had no desire to buy it, but my father was a contractor and had built many houses. He told me what he could do to the house once I bought it and encouraged me to fill out the paperwork and make an offer. I said ok with no interest and continued living my life. Then one day out of the blue, the realtor called and said I was approved.

My father made me take the $20k and put it down on the house. I did what he said because I got tired of the lectures and wanted to go back to having fun and living my social life. The next thing I knew, I was in the house. That place looked like nothing had been done to it since it was built. It had that old man smell and everything in there was old.

During this time, I was flying back and forth to D.C. because I had two offices, one there and the other in NY. I tried to stay in D.C. because I got tired of my father hounding me about the house. One day when I returned home, I was in shock. My father had knocked down some walls, finished the basement, and expanded the kitchen. It looked like a completely different house. The next week I started helping my father with the construction and added my personal touch to the rest.

My house was in the lily-white neighborhood of Westwood, NJ. I lived across the street from the Chief of Police and next door to him was the County Judge. Before I knew it, I was traveling out of town every week, and every week, I had a limo picking me up.

Eventually the Chief of Police found it necessary to introduce himself. I think his curiosity was kicking in. He came to my door to find out who I was and what I did for a living. I divulged that I was a music company executive and threw him some CDs to get him out of my way. However, he wasn't done with me. He offered to give me a PBA card, which is from the Police Benevolent Association. It is a card that many officers give family and friends as a "Don't go to jail" card if they are ever stopped. Well, I sure needed that because when I would enter into the town late at night, I was usually followed by a man in blue and was pulled over on more than one occasion.

The Chief admitted that my neighbors questioned who I was and suspiciously looked at me as a drug dealer. Him being a Black chief in a white town didn't stop the officers from pulling his son over so I was glad that he came over to be nosey because that card sure came in handy every time I got stopped. Let's just say that being in a nice neighborhood was nothing if you were there feeling like you were a target or being watched. I decided I would find something nice in a place where I could feel comfortable and free to roam, when the time came.

# CHAPTER 26

# IT'S TRICKY

As I transitioned into the promotions department, I had a chance to work with the O'Jays, one of my favorite groups. Eddie and I had already established a relationship early on when I toured with LeVert. His pride and admiration for his sons was touching and I never forgot how he would come out to watch them perform at every show.

Eddie and the O'Jays were signed to ABC Booking while I was an agent there and the bond that started years ago was rekindled. By the time I left ABC, they arrived at EMI with a record deal. It was a great reunion and we would always hang out when he would come to town. We still have a close friendship to this day.

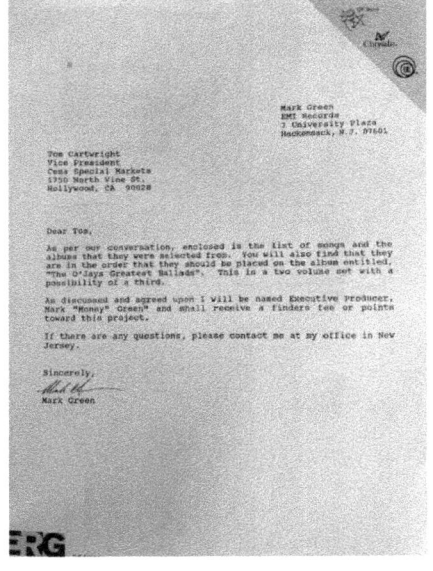

One day while on the road with Eddie, I shared that I was working on a project that was the O'Jays' greatest ballads, which was a mixed CD that played the records back-to-back without interruption. EMI loved the idea for the record, and they actually gave me a deal to complete the compilation. I needed one more song so I called one of my heroes, Kenny Gamble. I explained to Kenny what I was doing and expected him to give me his blessings. Unfortunately, as I was turning in the project I was told that Kenny took over the project. My idea now became his baby because he owned the masters. He snatched it right from under me.

I was beyond mad, angry and frustrated. Putting those three words together doesn't even explain the level of aggravation and ill feelings it caused me knowing that I trusted him. (*Rule #1: Trust No One*)

*Kenny Gamble & Mark Green*

I had been down this road so many times before in this business but each time, it was really disheartening and discouraging.

You want to be able to take someone at their word. You want to believe people are genuine and they certainly act like it until it's time for them to strike. It's hard for me to hold any ill feelings for a guy like Kenny who I looked up to and had studied everything about him and his company. Kenny is a legend and I still have the utmost respect for him. He was a mentor who I followed and watching him gave me great insight and guidance. However, I must say that this is the business I chose and many people are just in it for themselves. *(Rule #7: Never Underestimate the Other Person's Greed)*

I continued to move forward with my job as a regional promotions manager, because one thing I always did was to always keep on moving. One day while working at EMI, I was approached by someone in the street that asked if I would like to be in a movie. Of course, I said yes! They gave me an address and date to appear. When I showed up, I found out it was the Malcom X story. I was beyond ecstatic especially when I found out that Denzel Washington was the lead.

The movie was being produced and directed by Spike Lee, another favorite of mine. I was told to be at the location in Harlem to get set up and fitted for the movie. We were asked to be there at 9 a.m. When I arrived, we were in an event hall and all I could see were thousands of people. I could not believe all of those people were there for the same movie.

We were told to find a table and sit until we were called. As time passed, more and more people began to leave. By now it was 6 p.m. and I was ready to leave but I decided to wait it out. I had taken the week off from EMI and had nothing but time. Or so I thought.

As the clock got closer to 10 p.m., I began to pack my stuff when they called my table to the fitting room. After getting fitted, we were driven to the shoot location. I was excited and ready for the unknown. By now it was 1 a.m. and the streets were blocked off and the whole street had been changed to look like 1940. The street signs, the store fronts, and even the fire hydrants had been replaced and changed to meet the era.

As we moved onto the set, Spike Lee came in and he placed everyone in position. We filmed several shots but unfortunately, I was not in any of them.

The next day I decided to come at 6 p.m. when I knew that most people would leave because they had to work the next day or take care of their families. I brought some reading material and chopped it up with some folks there that were waiting for their chance at stardom. As 10 p.m. approached, we were called to get fitted. This time we went back to the same spot and Spike walked in and he placed everyone in location and once again, I was not in the shot. By now, I was beyond frustrated so I decided I would pay attention to where the camera was moving, so I could get caught in the shot. Every time I was placed, I would stay until Spike would leave the room. As soon as he was out of my view, I would drift over to the spot where the camera was panning, so I could make it in one of the shots.

On day five we got called at 11 p.m. to go to the set in Harlem. One of the PAs picked me and another woman to walk up and down 125th street in front of the Apollo, for the next shot. As the scene was being set, I ran into Oran "Juice" Jones. We knew each other from the record business so we chatted for a minute before they were ready to shoot. During the scene, Oran was walking up and down the street trying to sell watches when suddenly, he stopped in front of me for a small dialog. Well, I was not prepared, so when the cameras stopped right in front of me and within inches of my face, I froze like a deer in headlights.

The next thing I heard was "Cut! Let's shoot it again." Again he approached me and as I went to speak, the same thing happened. My mouth refused to form actual words.

"Cut!"

That was it. My very first speaking part in a movie down the drain.

That night I made friends with the PA and asked him to text me once he got on location so I could just come there instead of sitting for five hours just to get a shot. I broke him off with some duckets and took my outfit home. The next three to four days he would hit me up, and I would drive to the location, meet him, and he would walk me in on site. I got placed in all the scenes and as always, Spike would come in and place us where he wanted us to be. I began to wander from spot to spot until one of the last scenes we were shooting for the night was the scene where Malcom X is at the Podium and says, "You have been hoodwinked and bamboozled. Come and join me in Islam."

He is then approached by Brother Banes who walks him down the aisle and tells Malcolm that he wants to introduce him to Sister Betty Shabazz. As he is walking down the aisle, I am right there! Right in the crowd of people!

I stick my hand out and he shakes it just as he is greeted by Sister Betty Shabazz. At the end of the night, I didn't know if I made it into the scene or not. All I knew was that Denzel Washington shook my hand in the scene. I felt great!

*Mark Green on the set of "Malcolm X"*

The following days, I continued to show up at the time of the shoots and did what I always did—try to find the spot to stand for the next shot. The only other time I was close to being in a shot was when we were in the ballroom and a man yelled, "Get your hands out my pocket!" just before Malcom X is shot and killed. I returned one more week, but to be honest, the waiting game was frustrating. Not to mention, I had to get back to work.

Within the next couple of months, I was called to be an extra in two more movies, Sugar Hill starring Wesley Snipes and Michael Wright and another popular movie of that time that I can't recall. It was an experience of a lifetime. Nevertheless, it was very clear to me it was not my calling.

## CHAPTER 27

# WALK THIS WAY

As I returned to work, Glynice was restructuring the team, and she brought on a new hire. His name was Danny. Everyone was upset about her choice. He was an outsider who had not spent much time in our camp. Unfortunately, after about three years, he did a grimy move and stabbed Glynice in the back. He was behind her being fired. I became his next victim and met the same fate as Glynice. I was her ally which made me his adversary, so I had to go.

I had no job, but I wasn't stressin' it. I knew too many people and had been an upstanding businessman. I figured there had to be somebody that would help me change my current state of being in limbo. To my dismay, I was out there on my own. Nobody felt the camaraderie to lift me up, so I realized that friends in the entertainment industry are not the same as friends in your life. They could be here today and "not knowing you" tomorrow.

After trying and trying to get back "in the game," I had to fall back on what I went to college for. My degree was in Music

Education and I became a teacher at Rosa Parks Performing Arts High School in Paterson, NJ. I figured my music business career was something I would sit back and talk about when I got to the ripe age of sitting in my rocking chair. I constantly thought about all of my experiences and stayed in a state of nostalgia.

There was a student in my class who had an incredible voice, she was always singing and listening to a tape. I was curious about what she was listening to, and the more she sang in class, the more it felt like deja vu. It was like the biz was tapping me on the shoulder and whispering in my ear, every time I heard her melodic voice. I had to bet on my heart, my passion for music, and take a listen to her demo. It was a go!

I was going back in. I reached out to EMI and they weren't interested but as always, one monkey don't stop no show. I knew Ruben Rodriguez from working at EMI. Ruben had a label called Pendulum Records under EMI, and eventually signed the group to an album deal.

Divine's song, "Lately," hit number one on the pop charts and the girls became the opening act for Britney Spears while I returned to teaching feeling angry, frustrated, and mad at the world. Until I got a call from Dedra Tate who told me that Jeryl Busby (President of Motown) was looking for an executive to oversee his business venture. He had just bought into Flava Unit and needed someone brought in to represent him. I met with Jeryl and he hired me immediately.

After meeting with Shakim and Queen Latifah, I partnered up with Shakim on managing artists. The group I was assigned to manage was SWV. It was a great experience and we traveled worldwide to London, among other places internationally.

One day Shakim came to me and said we had to fly to L.A. to meet with this guy named Clarence Avant. I knew of him for two reasons. First because of his label and his background in music and second because I had just met this girl who I favored a lot. We went out on two dates

*Jeryl Busby, Shakim & Mark Green*

but out of the blue she said she was moving to L.A. to work for a guy name Clarence Avant. It would be years later that I heard she married a rapper named Eazy E.

I did not know the urgency to meet up with Clarence because I did not know who he really was at the time. However, he was very humble and offered me his card and told me to call him if I ever needed anything. Looking back on the situation it was a missed opportunity.

Shakim and I got along great. He liked that I was laid back like him and could handle multiple tasks. Shakim was a great manager and I watched his every move. He had his plate full just dealing with Faith Evans, who had just had a baby with

Biggie, Naughty by Nature, who was driving him crazy, and all of the other artists he had to deal with, not to mention his main client, Queen Latifah. As I got more and more into management, I began to understand Shakim's frustration and although at times I wanted to turn into the monster that was breathing inside of me, I continued to remind myself of past experiences of just speaking my mind and not carefully selecting my words.

## CHAPTER 28

# OMG

As soon as we returned back to New York with SWV, we hit the road again traveling to Houston for promos at the radio stations and also visiting record stores. At one record store, a guy came up to me talking about his girl group. He was very passionate and persistent. It was almost like he would not take no for an answer. He gave me the demo and his business card and continued to talk about the girl group. It was not until five or more years later that I realized who he was, but first I had to make sure. So, I went through all my business cards until I found that card. I looked at the card and read the name and I couldn't believe that I missed that opportunity. His name was Matthew Knowles, and the group he was begging me to listen to happened to be his daughter's group and her name was Beyoncé.

SWV was hotter than any R&B group at the time and we did everything from Soul Train to London's Top of the Charts TV Show. The week we were on our way to London, I invited my friend Red to come on the road with us. I was going to use him as a bodyguard. Red had gotten caught up in the crack scene and I felt bad for him. He was a good dude who always looked out for me and had my back, so I wanted to help him get back on his feet. I started calling him towards the end of the week to make sure he was ready but I never got a call back. Red never made it on the tour with us because he lost his life that weekend.

I was devastated that I couldn't make it to the funeral. Thinking back on it though, he had gotten me into so many sticky situations and put my name in the middle of his drama so many times that I wouldn't have been surprised if some of the people he had robbed or owed money to may have come after me to settle his debts. I was already receiving phone calls from thugs and gangsters looking for him. Running with Red had put red dots on my head, literally, and a target on my back. I just had to pray he would make it into the pearly gates.

My fondest, or should I say scariest, moment with him was when I decided to visit him in Chicago. When I got to Chicago, he asked me to rent a car. This was unusual because Red always had a luxury car waiting for me. I had the O'Jays there for a show and I arrived in a suit and tie and proceeded to rent the car. The only car they had was an Impala, so I took it.

Red told me he had to make a stop so he directed me to an apartment complex and told me to wait in the car. At the time I didn't know I was at Cabrini Green projects in Chicago. He went upstairs to get his "fix" and I was in the rented car that looked like a detective's cruiser. When I looked up and saw at least four lasers on my forehead, I thought I was about to meet my maker. It dawned on me that the car looked like I was stakin' out the area or about to do surveillance. I really could have been taken out, just like that. Thank God we got out of there safely with product in hand.

The next day we went to Red's condo which was across the street from the Oprah Winfrey television show. When I got to the condo, I noticed it was totally bare. There was no furniture, no beds, no dishes, clothes, or towels. I decided to go to the store to make some purchases. As I left, I realized I had no key to get back in, so I went in the garbage, got some paper and stuck it in the door so it would not lock and I could return. After I returned to the condo, we were eating and having small talk when we heard a loud bang at the door. As soon as Red heard that knock he went into a shock. I had never seen him look scared all the days of my life. He pulled me to the side and asked me how I got back into the condo. I informed him about the paper in the door but I did not remove it. He was horrified and said not to move. The banging got louder and it didn't sound like a hand at all, but more like a gun handle. We sat in silence and frozen stiff for more than an hour until we felt the coast was clear. When there was no seeming presence of anyone outside, I jumped up, took my chances, and ran out of there like my hair was on fire!

These were the type of "episodes" I would have with Red. And it wasn't the first or last time. Rest in Peace Red, you lived your life to the fullest!

Although I hate to say it, *the show must go on* as always, so we went overseas, and it was a successful tour. I enjoyed the experience with SWV, and I became close with LeLee and remain good friends with her today.

It wasn't long before Jeryl Busby decided to pull out of the company, and I soon followed, however not by choice. They let me go just as fast as he said he was out.

## CHAPTER 29

# U GOT IT BAD

After leaving Flavor Unit, I reminded Jeryl that I needed a job. He had taken me from my teaching job and I was back to being unemployed. He asked me to reach back out and he would take care of me. I chased him down for two weeks but of course, nothing ever happened. *(Rule #2: Don't Believe the Hype!)*

The year was 1995 and I was out of work and did what I could always do… "road trippin." It seems like no matter what happened and how many positions I held at any given time, I always received a call to return to the business of touring at the most needed times. A guy named Mark Cheatham called me and asked if I would go out on the road with an artist named Usher. Usher had just come out and was new to the game. I was his second road manager and working with him was cool but game recognizes game and our birthdays were one day apart so let's just say, I was an older version of him and "I let him live" because he was young and having fun.

Usher had a good work ethic. He wasn't a knucklehead and was respectable. I wasn't loose with him, but I had to keep him under wraps as his road manager because he was like a young prince who was about to take the throne, and it was my job to make sure nothing happened to him.

One night in particular he asked me to go out and I just felt that it wasn't a good idea, so I knew he didn't like me to be able to tell him no...but I had to do it. As a road manager, you must sometimes be able to see into the future and instead of having to clean up a mess after it's over, avoid letting a situation get messy at all. I was good at what I did. And I say that humbly.

*Usher & Mark Green*

We were backstage on another night and after the show, an altercation took place. I had let one thing slide too long and it almost bit me in the butt. Usher had a bodyguard that he must have had some history with or a personal relationship with that would allow him to allow the bodyguard to look after him. I say that because the bodyguard could only "half" look after him. I am making a disclaimer that I have no animosity or desire to ridicule anyone who is handicapped. But to be honest, some jobs require certain things and I do believe that a bodyguard should have sight in both eyes. Right?

Well, this one had one good eye and another eye that was covered with a "Slick Rick" patch.

When the fight broke out, the bodyguard had a hard time maintaining the situation. Thank God things were resolved without any casualties or bad injuries. But it was interesting watching him turn his whole body around to see what was going on. I felt bad knowing that at any time, he could have been taken out without his knowledge. His situation did not sit well with me but I was new to the camp and I needed to assess my situation before making changes.

No sooner than finishing Usher's tour, I was contracted to jump on another one. This time it was with Missy Elliott. I had so many people calling on me to go out on the road with them, that I had to form a company. I revived the name and started "On Cue Touring Productions." I hired four other managers and gave them the tours that I couldn't be part of. Missy Elliott, Timbaland, Backstreet Boys and 3LW were the acts.

*3LW & Mark Green*

During the 3LW tour, I went out a couple of times with them, including the time they went on tour with NSync. They were managed by a girl who I introduced to the entertainment game. She had just graduated from Yale and was working for IBM when we met. She had a strong interest in getting into this business. We spent time together as she met some of my colleagues who schooled her on the tricks of the trade. It did not take long before she was running things in the record business, and she rose quickly to the top.

I have always been the type of person to want to help people who genuinely have a passion for the business, but at the same time, I have found that when people get where they are trying to go, they sometimes forget who was instrumental in getting them there. Looking back, I was so concerned about moving my company forward that I did not get to spend quality time with the acts with which I was touring. I was hired by Louise West the super attorney who is responsible for many successful executives and artist including myself. She knew talent, hits, and had a gangsta pen game going that made her stand out amongst the best attorneys in the game. At the time, Mona Scott was managing Missy and

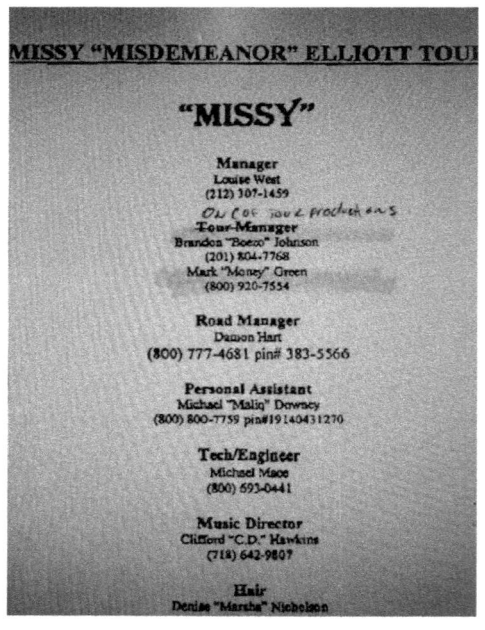

although I had the opportunity of visiting her at her house, we never really developed a relationship. I spent more time dealing with Louise, her attorney, and Missy's mother.

Timbaland was another protege of Louise West and made a big name for himself. He was a dope producer but he, on the other hand, wanted to be more. He wanted to be an artist as well. As we began to build our relationship, he asked to meet with me in NY to discuss his plans for his career. He asked to meet him at a club that he and Justin Timberlake were allegedly looking into buying. When I got there, he was with Justin and his then-girlfriend, Cameron Diaz. Everyone was in a party mood—drinking, smoking, and having a great time. I, on the other hand, was in a business mood and found it hard to conduct business in that manner. However, we created a plan and I was ready for the opportunity. Timbaland had expressed his desire to be an artist similar to Puffy where he would produce and perform. So, I took it all in and began to book his tour.

I was excited! Here was an opportunity to make him a mega star as a performer. I had studied Puffy and his humble beginning and I knew exactly what I needed to do. My first chance came when I booked Timbaland to headline a major festival in London. He was excited about the opportunity as well, until I got that fatal phone call that would change the trajectory of our relationship. He

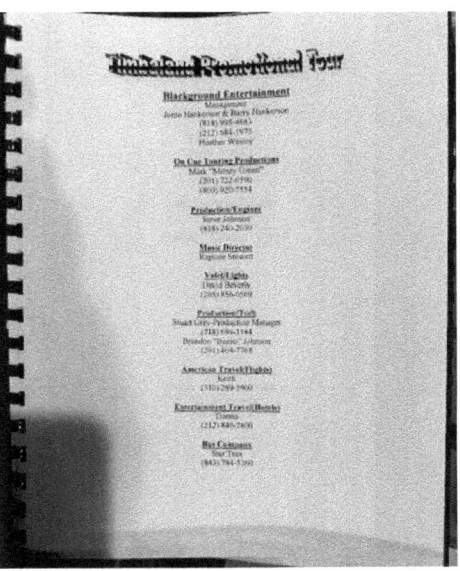

said, "I have to cancel the tour date because I'm working with this new artist, Alicia Keys, and I need to stay put and finish the project." I was beyond mad, angry, and frustrated. I'd just put all my effort into creating an opportunity and he pulled out! Not to mention I had already paid him in full. I was not concerned about getting the money back because we both shared the same lawyer, Louise West. So, Louise drafted the paperwork, and I received the money but never had another opportunity to work with him again. It also caused me to lose my relationship with my London promoter. Lesson learned. *(Rule #5: C.R.E.A.M.)*

Next, I got an opportunity to work with a group from France, Les Nubians. I enjoyed working with them and loved their music but I couldn't understand a word they were saying because they spoke French. Their hit song was Makeda. I loved that song from the first time I heard it and was excited to work with the sisters. We spent the first half of the tour traveling to cities that had a large French connection like Canada, Washington D.C., Boston, etc. It was an exciting time for me learning the culture and trying to speak French. I did learn a little bit of the language. Parlez-vous Francais?

*Les Nubians*

## CHAPTER 30

# MAKE EM SAY UHH

In my pursuit of my next position, I came across a company called Tru Tone. It was a record pressing plant. I was familiar with them along with other record plants. I felt strong about my interview because I knew the game so I was ready and willing! During my interview, I was told I had to find clients who would pay to have their records pressed up and who would be interested in starting their own record labels. It sounded good, but I thought, "How many people like that could I find that would allow me to have a steady and livable income?"

Master P had become the poster boy for selling products out of your trunk and getting rich. He gave the average rapper or person with dreams of running their own company the spark to believe that if he could do it, they could too. Let's just say, the job wasn't as bad as I had believed that it would be. I began to get calls from everywhere.

Melba Moore, Teena Marie, The O'Jays, JT Taylor of Kool and the Gang, and an NFL player from the NY Giants were a few of the people who called and wanted to have their own label. I also got calls from drug dealers who really thought they could take the Master P blueprint to the bank. I entertained them all. By the time I was finished, I was being offered jobs by the same people who were hiring me to start their business.

I was offered a job by JT Taylor to run his label. I took it although I did not leave my position at Tru Tone. I was excited that he'd asked me to be part of his company because I grew up with JT in the same town. When I was younger, he had a band called Filet of Soul and I would travel around town just to watch him sing. He was a star in the making back in the day and it seemed fitting for him to continue with Kool & The Gang as the lead singer. Things were going well and we were making a lot of progress. JT had just left Kool and the Gang and he was responsible for their big comeback in the 90's with all the hits he wrote like "Ladies Night,"

*Chris Webber & Mark Green*

"Get Down on it," "Celebration," and many more! But then I got a fateful call from Glynice with an offer I could not refuse.

Glynice asked me to come and help her with the label that was owned by the NBA All-Star, Chris Webber of the Sacramento Kings. He wasn't just an NBA player, he wanted to rap! Rap really had people feeling powerful enough to change the world. Chris' manager was Stacy Murray. We had worked together at Capitol Records and knew each other well. Stacy was not a shy or timid woman. She was fierce and demanding. She didn't take any shit and nobody really tested her because of it.

While I was working with JT, we had finished his first solo project after leaving Kool and the Gang. He was determined to be a solo artist. However, I had to change focus as Chris called for more of my time. I had to part ways with JT and focus on Chris' label, Humility Records. Besides, the money Chris was offering put me back in the game financially.

Everything was fine during the basketball off-season. We worked closely together. But when the season started, he became a ghost. We never saw him. We would sit in the office as everything sat at a standstill. It was like playing Freeze Tag and nobody came to unfreeze you to let you move again. We had to wait until Chris was available to okay the projects or whatever else he was in charge of.

We finally brought it to his attention that we felt like sitting ducks when he wasn't around and initially he would make himself available to meet with us by flying us all over the country. But even with that, nothing really changed. I had brought an idea about a project to Chris one day and he liked the idea. Liking it didn't get it done. Nothing came out of the meeting. I was beginning to get bored at the slow-moving company. I was used to the hustle and bustle, not sitting and waiting for someone to say, "Go."

## CHAPTER 31

# THIS IS MY CONFESSION

That's when I got a call from Usher. He asked me to come back and work as his road manager again. It was 1997 and Usher was no longer a little boy who was a rookie but now he was an established artist who had some hits under his belt. He knew exactly what he wanted and how he wanted his brand to be represented. I would watch Usher rehearse day and night. He was determined to be the next big thing in

On Cue Touring Productions
79 Palisade Ave., Westwood N.J. 07605 (201) 722-0590

**"USHER"**

**On Cue Tour Productions**
Mark "Money" Green
(201) 722-0590
(800) 920-7554

Brandon "Beezo" Johnson
(201) 646-9797
(201) 804-7768
cell(201) 650-5306

**Booking Agent**
**I.C.M.**
Mark Cheatam
(212) 556-5753

**Manager**

R&B. Usher would spend hours rehearsing and dancing in the mirror and then he would work out doing sit-ups, push-ups, and more. He was totally focused and determined to take over the game. The other male R&B artists or groups at the time were the "King of Pop" Michael Jackson, R. Kelly, Keith Sweat, Babyface, and Tevin Campbell. Out of the seven of them, Usher was holding his own with the giants. He was not at all a one hit wonder, nor did he drift off into oblivion.

One day while on tour in Nashville, Usher asked me to take him to the mall. We went into a store and a few people recognized him. I didn't think anything of it. As we continued to stroll the mall like regular folk, a crowd had begun formulating and it was growing larger and larger (about 100 people). I started to get anxious. I knew that something that could start out as innocent and flattering to the "star" could quickly turn dangerous.

I told him we had to go but I urged him not to run. As we were leaving, an older mall security guard observed the movement towards us and without knowing what was really going on, thought he was able to stop the situation from getting out of hand by grabbing Usher by the arm. I immediately pushed his hand off of Usher as we continued to swiftly make our way out of there. I told Usher

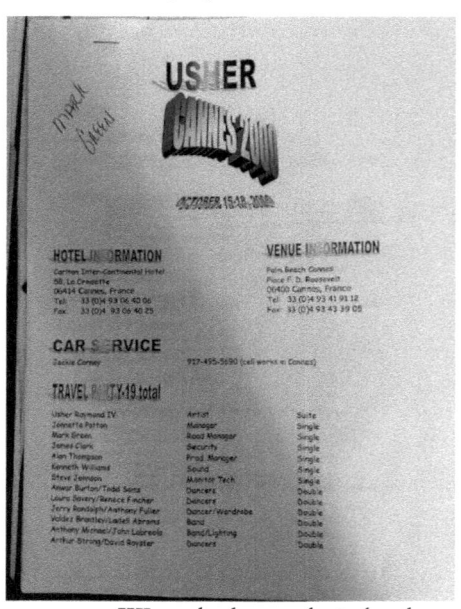

again to walk fast but not to run. We calmly made it back to the car and the epiphany that he had "made it" showed up. That had to be one of the scariest moments though. Imagine a couple hundred people following you, yelling, and trying to get close to you to get a photo.

Usher figured that since we would be working together, it would be best and cost effective to move me to Atlanta. He put me up in an apartment for three months. We spent most of our time rehearsing for this big event in Paris, France. There was so much to deal with between applying for work permits, shipping equipment, booking flights, rehearsals, making sure everyone's visas were in order, and the daily responsibility of preparing for a major concert, that I didn't have a moment to myself to do anything else.

One thing I noticed as his star elevated, was that he did not become lackadaisical or lazy. He did not think that he didn't have to work hard anymore. He actually became more demanding. He wanted things to be perfect and his way.

When we arrived in France, it was about 4 a.m. their time and about 7 p.m. eastern. Usher called me and requested spaghetti. I tried to do what I always do, which is take care of my artists and get them whatever they desire but it was also 4 a.m.

I attempted to get him the meal that he was craving by calling room service. They had already received the same request from Usher and had already informed him that they had no sauce and given the time, everything was already closed. I had attempted to even pay them to send someone to the store to get what Usher asked for but we were not in the "city that never sleeps." Certain places went to bed and there was just no way to get him spaghetti at that ungodly hour.

Usher kept calling me about the damn spaghetti. I was not in the mood to go on a wild goose chase after flying for hours on an international flight with a whole group of people that I had to keep up with, keep in line, and keep together. I finally told the chef to give him some ketchup in a bowl and take it to his room. I then proceeded to turn off my phone.

I took my chances because at the end of the day, I tried. In situations like this, things can go awry because a celebrity is a celebrity. They are not "normal" people. They live extraordinary lives and not taking anything from them, most of the ones who are successful, work hard to entertain us. They do sometimes get backlash for having outrageous demands. I am just glad that Usher woke up the next day and didn't have any gripes with me. I guess the ketchup tasted like Ragu at four in the morning.

Great news met us on the arrival back into the U.S. when he was awarded the opening act for the Janet Jackson tour. That is why I loved and still love this business because there is never a dull moment.

We were ready to get it on and poppin' with "Miss Jackson if you're nasty" on her Velvet Rope tour. I was excited and everyone else was too. Usher's dreams were coming true and then the needle scratched the record when my phone rang and I heard Chris Webber's voice on the other end. I knew he wouldn't be just calling to say, "What's up."

## CHAPTER 32

# SQUARE BIZ

Chris Webber had a job for me to do and it was to put a party together for All-Star Weekend in New York City. I had no choice but to leave the tour because I was on payroll for Chris and at the time, he was paying me $75k, which was a lot back then. So I left the tour. As I was beginning to put together all of the events for All-Star Weekend, things fell through. I had started to redirect my energy to the party when he pulled the plug. I was more than frustrated even knowing these things sometimes happen in this business. I just wish I could have experienced touring with Miss Jackson.

Besides playing basketball, Chris was still working on his album. I, on the other hand, when not working in the office, was in the studio with the producers working on the music. All of a sudden, the NBA went on strike and Chris had to put a hold on his music endeavors. He asked us to take a hiatus, indefinitely. Which meant our paychecks came to a halt. Chris had just signed a deal for $70 million so I could not understand why he could not continue to pay us.

All of that took me back to focusing on me again. I always had passion projects that I would try to get done when I wasn't working on someone else's career. I reached out to the Warner Brothers executive who gave Chris his deal. I presented a four-album project, involving Teena Marie, JT Taylor, The O'Jays, and Melba Moore.

The idea was to sell at least 100 thousand units, which would put a nice piece of change in my pocket. The record executive loved the idea and the first artist up was Teena Marie. I didn't personally know Teena but a colleague named Stuart Gray had worked with her and Rick James and he put me in touch with her. I had always been a big fan of hers and this was definitely a dream come true.

Teena and I met up in Philly at one of her concerts. We had been talking on the phone for about a month and I could not wait to meet her. As soon as we met, we began planning the project. We were months into planning when she presented her album to me. I was bummed when I didn't hear anything that I felt would be a hit. How could I tell one of my favorite artists that she didn't have a hit? We finally came up with a song to release as a single. In the meantime, we stayed in communication. We were always on the phone talking about music, life, love, and sometimes, Rick James. Whenever she would come into town, we would meet up. She would always call and invite me to her shows.

One day we had a long, deep conversation that covered everything you could think of. We talked about Rick James. We talked about our music careers. She talked about her life and what she still wanted to accomplish in it. One thing she expressed was that she absolutely despised drugs and the drug scene. Rick James had already passed away but she expressed the pain of dealing with him and his drug use. She also knew that some of the members of her band were getting high and although she didn't like it, there really wasn't much she could do about it. Then we discussed her daughter who was still young at the time. Teena never liked to leave her daughter to go on the road. We also had a long talk about death and Teena was a Christian and she had her business in order unlike many other artists. She had a will and a plan.

I was so ecstatic about our record contract that I publicized it before the record came out. That was not a smart move because Cash Money Records saw my interview in *Sister to Sister* magazine and called her and offered her a lot of money to sign with them and she did. The amount that I offered her was no comparison to their money or the song "Still in Love" that they had produced for her that became a hit.

Teena asked me to release her from her contract and although I didn't want to, I did it out of respect for who she was and her being one of my favorite artists. Had it been someone else, I don't think I would have reacted so kindly. I allowed my emotions to overrule my business sense. *(Rule #10: Trust Your Gut and Not Your Feelings)*

Shortly after her album was released, the Warner Brothers executive was not happy about the decision I'd made, so that put a wedge between us and my deal dissolved along with the other artists I had scheduled for distribution.

After the release of her Cash Money cd, we would hook up again. This time I booked Teena at Bergen Pac in Englewood to perform. I brought her in two days early hoping to spend some time with her. However, I did not have her current number and asked her road manager to call her and let her know it was my show.

The day of the show I informed Teena that she was less than one mile from my house and I had brought her in early so we could spend some time together and work on her projects. She was so angry to find out that we were so close in proximity and no one told her that it was my show. She expressed to me that she would have come over to my house. We could have visited some radio stations and just hung out in the city, but instead she was stuck in a lonely, boring hotel room for two days.

*Teena Marie & Mark Green*

On the day of the show, I went to pay the road manager and she requested cash. I informed her that as a non-profit and a company, we were not allowed to pay performers in cash. She was not happy but took the check. After the show, I expressed to Teena my apologies for not paying her in cash and she asked me what I was talking about. "I never do cash," she said. This added another layer of frustration she had with her road manager. However, the real shocker came when she told me she didn't know what the gig was paying. "How could you not know?" I asked her. She informed me that she trusted her road manager who had been with her for forever and she relied on her for all of the details. I could not believe what I heard from a woman who was so smart and organized. But I could relate because I had been burned many times before, by people who I thought I could trust. *(Rule #1: Trust No One)*

The news of her death was a shocker. I was devastated and hurt when I heard of her passing. I still can't believe she is gone. Every time I hear her music it brings such joy to my heart to know that I had the pleasure of working and hanging with one of R&Bs greats!

Her dying from a seizure reminded me of one of our conversations about medicine, holistic medicine, and herbal regiments. She did not like to take medication. At the time of her death, she had finished her fourteenth studio album. She was only fifty-four years old when she died. Like many other artists who died rather young, she was gone too soon.

## CHAPTER 33

# IN MY BED

It was not long before I was contacted by my good friend, Keith Ingram, to go on the road with a new group called Dru Hill. The group consisted of four male singers from Baltimore, Maryland. Keith was from Baltimore and had signed the group to management along with a guy name Kevin Peck. After my meeting with Kevin and Keith, I sat down with Sisqo and the other members of the group to discuss their goals, ideas, and to listen to their dreams and where they wanted to be in their career. I sometimes called myself the dream maker because I love to make dreams come true and in a blink of an eye, another star was born.

Sisqo's work ethic reminded me of Usher. He was very hard working. He was always trying to perfect his craft. Sisqo was clearly a star. It was apparent from the very beginning, and I was interested in seeing where they were going. I met with Kevin and Keith and introduced them to the "road game" and showed them the ropes on how to have a successful tour.

I did what I customarily do when I sit down with a new artist or group. I got acquainted with them because we would be traveling together and having a good rapport with my clients was key. I cannot sit here and say that all you have to do is ask someone what they like and provide it for them. But it was my job to hear, see, and be able to help the artist(s) fulfill their dreams. We may not always become the best of friends on tour, but respect and professionalism go a long way.

We discussed the songs in the show, the run of show, and I came up with the idea to bring out an actual bed on stage for the song "In My Bed." The scenario would involve Sisqo having a girl in the bed and while he was singing, there would be an insinuation that "somebody was sleeping in his bed" as the song states.

A few of the shows had this "set" and when the song was coming to a close, the stage would go black, and you'd hear a gunshot, and the audience would assume that there was actually someone in the bed and Sisqo handled it by taking the guy out. It was all good until the Women's Rights groups and organizations that worked against domestic violence caught a whiff of the stage performance and flexed their muscles. We definitely had to change the scene.

The tour began in August and finished in the first week of October. We were on tour with Mary J. Blige, Ginuwine, Aaliyah, Bone Thugs & Harmony, and Kid Capri. Pierre the Comedian hosted the show.

It was one of my favorite tours—amazing! However, like always, there had to be some drama. During a segment of the tour, one of the crew members had asked me if two girls that he was with could change their clothes in my suite, and I said yes. I had no idea what else they had in mind.

By the time I came out to the living room to greet them and be cordial, they were already preparing to turn my room into a crack den. They had all of the supplies, paraphernalia, and the determination to get "beamed up to Scotty" as we used to say. I had to halt them from boarding the spaceship. I told the crew to take them to another "launching pad" because those kinds of festivities were not going to take place in my room. I thought the problem was solved until I did my rounds.

Two hours later I knocked on another room door and when the door opened, they were back from space and looking like the "Night of the Walking Dead." They were so high that they were walking around the room butt-naked and out of sorts. It was a mess to see people transform from normal to "cracked all the way out." Considering this was the era of crack and cocaine, anything was possible. I could not believe that two of my crew guys had taken part in the pipe dream activities. After they came down from cloud nine, we had a talk and it never happened again.

We made a stop in Detroit, Michigan and had a show there. During that time, a representative from Pelle Pelle came to present the opportunity for us to look at their new line of leather jackets as that was the "it" name to have on your back at that time. They sent us into the warehouse and told us we could get whatever we wanted. We were grabbing everything we could in sight. Part of the collaboration was for them to have a photo shoot with Dru Hill as a marketing campaign, wearing their designs.

The campaign was so successful that their sales skyrocketed to the highest since the establishment of their company. It was so good that I got a job as a marketing and product placement manager for Pelle Pelle that lasted for three years. I had the opportunity to style and dress several artists such as Jagged Edge, Juvenile, AJ from BET, and many more. You couldn't tell me I wasn't the man with every different "flavor" and color of Pelle Pelle jackets than you can imagine. I had so many that I was giving them away.

During the last leg of the tour, we were in Oklahoma City, and they had just finished performing a show. We were traveling from Oklahoma to Denver and the bus driver decided to bypass one of many signs that directed buses and trucks to randomly pull over to willingly get searched for drugs and contraband. Sounds crazy, don't it? I mean, who is going to just stop to get searched especially when you don't see a police car in your view? The bus driver obviously felt that way because he did not pull over and told me later that it was because he assumed there were probably drugs on the bus that he didn't have anything to do with.

I honestly didn't see the sign but when we were pulled over by damn near a whole police department and then some, I was shocked when the officer who wanted to speak to the "man in charge," (me) told me we were being stopped for that reason.

I told the officer that I didn't see the sign for one, I wasn't the one driving for two, and three, I was traveling with Dru Hill. Once he said he wasn't familiar with the group, I painted them as gospel singers. They really were clean and stand up "kids" who just wanted to sing, be famous, and live out their dreams.

When we passed the sign, I didn't notice it but I did notice that something was going on when the Oklahoma City police department, the county police, and the state troopers were following us in full force. They must have had every on and off duty cop called in because they looked like a funeral procession with their lights and sirens glaring and wailing behind us. It looked like a traveling Christmas show.

Once they pulled us over, they made everyone besides me and a crew member walk to the top of a hill that was off from the highway and buses. They wanted to speak with us, without an entourage getting involved.

The first thing they asked me was if we had drugs on the bus and I confidently said no. I thought we were good. They went on the bus and found a bag of weed in the garbage. That is until one of the crew members came to whisper in my ear and inform me that there was some weed on the bus. The crew member told them that some girls left

| DATE | DAY | CITY | VENUE |
|---|---|---|---|
| | | **DRU HILL TOUR 1997** | |
| | | 1997 - MARY J. BLIGE / BONE THUGS-N-HARMONY | |
| 8/23 | SAT | LAST DAY OF REHEARSAL | PACK CASES FOR TOUR |
| 8/24 | SUN | ************** | ************OFF*************** |
| 8/25 | MON | EQUIPMENT TRUCK DEPARTS FOR | BUFFALO NY FROM SYR SYRACUSE N |
| 8/26 | TUES | EQUIPMENT LOAD IN MARINE MIDLAND ARENA BUFFALO NY | LOAD IN TIME 11:00AM |
| 8/27 | WED | BUS DEPARTS FROM MONTANA STUDIO AT 10:00AM FOR BUFFALO | HOTEL CHECK IN BAND/DANCERS AT 8:00PM |
| 8/28 | THUR | BUFFALO NY | MARINE MIDLAND ARENA |
| 8/29 | FRI | CLEVELAND OH | GUND ARENA |
| 8/30 | SAT | PHILADELPHIA PA | CORE STATES CENTER |
| 8/31 | SUN | WASHINGTON DC | US AIR ARENA |
| 9/1 | MON | CHARLOTTE NC | COLISEUM |
| 9/2 | TUES | ***********TRAVEL/OFF*********** | ***********TRAVEL/OFF*********** |
| 9/3 | WED | MEMPHIS TENN | PYRAMID ARENA |
| 9/4 | THURS | NASHVILLE TENN | ARENA |
| 9/5 | FRI | DETROIT MI | PALACE |
| 9/6 | SAT | CHICAGO ILL | UNITED CENTER |
| 9/7 | SUN | DAYTON OH | NUTTER CENTER |
| 9/8 | MON | ***********TRAVEL/OFF*********** | ***********TRAVEL/OFF*********** |
| 9/9 | TUES | ***********TRAVEL/OFF*********** | ***********TRAVEL/OFF*********** |
| 9/10 | WED | ATLANTA GA | LAKEWOOD AMPHITHEA |
| 9/11 | THURS | BALTIMORE MD | CIVIC ARENA |
| 9/12 | FRI | NY NY | MADISON SQUARE GARDEN |
| 9/13 | SAT | HARTFORD CONN | CIVIC CENTER |
| 9/14 | SUN | WORCESTER MASS | CENTRUM |
| 9/15 | MON | ***********TRAVEL/OFF*********** | ***********TRAVEL/OFF*********** |
| 9/16 | TUES | ***********TRAVEL/OFF*********** | ***********TRAVEL/OFF*********** |
| 9/17 | WED | PITTSBURG PA | CIVIC ARENA |
| 9/18 | THURS | HAMPTON VA | COLISEUM |
| 9/19 | FRI | GREENSBORO NC | COLISEUM |
| 9/20 | SAT | ORLANDO FL | CENTROPLEX ARENA |
| 9/21 | SUN | MIAMI FL | ARENA |
| 9/22 | MON | ***********TRAVEL/OFF*********** | ***********TRAVEL/OFF*********** |
| 9/23 | TUES | OKLAHOMA CITY OK | MYRAD |
| 9/24 | WED | DENVER COLORADO | McNICHOLS ARENA |
| 9/25 | THURS | ***********TRAVEL/OFF*********** | ***********TRAVEL/OFF*********** |
| 9/26 | FRI | HOUSTON TX | THE SUMMIT |
| 9/27 | SAT | ST. LOUIS MO | KEIL CENTER |
| 9/28 | SUN | DALLAS TX | REUNION ARENA |
| 9/29 | MON | ***********TRAVEL/OFF*********** | ***********TRAVEL/OFF*********** |
| 9/30 | TUES | ***********TRAVEL/OFF*********** | ***********TRAVEL/OFF*********** |
| 10/1 | WED | SEATTLE WASH | KEY ARENA |
| 10/2 | THUR | SACRAMENTO CA | ARCU ARENA |
| 10/3 | FRI | SAN JOSE CA | ARENA |
| 10/4 | SAT | LOS ANGELES CA | THE FORUM |
| 10/5 | SUN | PHOENIX AZ | ARIZONA COLIS OR DESERT SKY |

that on the bus from the last show.

While the police officer searched the bus, I got this information and I guess I figured the weed wouldn't be as bad as something else but lo and behold, he told me that he also had a small package of cocaine in one of the keyboard boxes.

Luckily it was in the third luggage bay of the bus. So, while the officer was checking the inside of the bus with the sniffing dog, I found one officer that seemed to be a groupie and I tried to use him as a decoy to take the attention off of the bus, and to the "celebrities" that were present. I got Dru Hill to come down and start signing autographs. I was hoping this would cool the officer's jets and have them call off the search before they made it to that last storage bin where they would surely find the cocaine.

The officers were getting curious as to why we were there, where we were going, and they were hoping to make a score on us. Although they hadn't heard of Dru Hill, when I mentioned that we were traveling with Bone, Thugs & Harmony, they surely knew them and figured that their bus would be a big score.

To prove my point, when I mentioned Bone, Thugs & Harmony, the officer said, "We know they get high, because we have seen their videos." They let us go and I am not sure if anything happened to the group, but I doubt it because they were at the next show. So, like many other times, it was a close call and now a memory that I can laugh about. But as always, *the show must go on!*

We had a few isolated dates after that including a

nightclub in Atlanta. One of Dru Hill's managers got into a fight with the brother of the President of Island Records, a division of PolyGram Records. During the fight, someone brandished a gun and shortly thereafter, the police arrived. Dru Hill ended up filing a lawsuit against the President of Island Records. Their complaint expressed Dru Hill's desire to get out of their record contract and the fact that further violence had been threatened against them, making them feel like they were not going to be in a safe working environment.

Basically, the fight turned into a melee and there became bad blood between Dru Hill and their label so they wanted out. During the deposition, some unfavorable words were exchanged, and it seemed to be proven that the working relationship would continue to be hostile after the incident. The judge awarded a settlement that was worth seven figures and that's all that I'm going to say.

*Dru Hill & Mark Green*

I will end it by saying that whenever money, ego, image, and entertainment are involved, there is always the chance of an explosion. Sometimes your mouth can buy you into a situation that your checking account will have to cash you out of.

After the tour ended, it was back to call waiting, waiting for that next phone call. I had no job and figured that the next gig would be finding me soon. I was right. A former record company executive called and asked me to do independent promotions. It was a first, dealing with artists who were trying to get their records "spun" on air. Let's just say to get a record played, you have to either have a powerful label who can flex their muscles and get what they want or you can have an independent promotion person to get your music played "by any means necessary."

CHAPTER 34

# IN DA CLUB

Doing independent promotions was no issue for me. Hell, I had participated in everything this business had to offer. So, I had no problem rolling up to a radio station with a paper bag or a pocket full of items. Whatever I needed to get my records played, I got them played. I think the fact that I was laidback and unassuming was the reason that people had no problem dealing with me or accepting my gifts.

One day I ran into a guy who worked at one of the NY stations. He was an on-air DJ and he and I hit it off right from the beginning. We were like two peas in a pod and would just hang night after night. Everywhere we went, he would always have a man bag with him. One night I pulled him to the side and asked what was in it? He opened it up and banished a nine. I looked at him and laughed and pulled up my shirt to show him my .380. That moment just bonded us even more.

After he would get off the air, we would head up to Harlem and run through the clubs, always ending at some after-hour spot. There was always drugs, money, and trouble awaiting us. On one occasion we were in an after-hour spot when a fight broke out and the sound of gunfire hit the air. We ran out of that place like it was on fire. One late night we were leaving one club and ended up in another club called the "Book" in Harlem. It was a well-known after-hour spot where the likes of LT and other celebrities would sometimes show up. As night got closer to day, people would smoke weed and socialize. I felt ashamed because when I was leaving, people were on their way to church. I could not believe I had stayed in that club until 10 a.m. That was the last time I went to that club, or any other club, and stayed until morning.

After a while, I got used to walking around with a gun on me. It was no different than carrying a wallet until one day, my life almost changed for the worse. I was on 7th Ave in NYC with a friend who worked at Capitol Records. We were headed somewhere when I got run off the road by a taxi driver and my car ended up on the sidewalk. The taxi was at a red light so I jumped out of my car to approach the driver. As soon as I got to the window, he pulled out a bat. I ran back to my car to get my gun and as I headed towards him, I heard my friend Tanya yell, "Don't do it! You are going to ruin your life! It's not worth it!" A bell went off in my head and I turned and walked back to my car. It was that day that I decided never to carry a gun again.

Early one morning I was at home when my friend from the radio station got into a dispute with his girl and ended up in jail. He called to ask for some duckets and I sent him what I had to help him get out. When he got out, I noticed that he had begun to change. He was living this "gangsta lifestyle" and was taking it too seriously. For me, it was all fun and games. I had no desire to be *that guy*. As I began to focus on my life, our relationship started to disintegrate. It was not long before he informed me he got a job in D.C. as a DJ. I was so happy for him because he needed a new start, away from NYC.

After he got settled in, he invited me down to D.C. I stayed at his place and would wait for him to finish work so we could hit the clubs. Like always, he would shout me out on the radio, and I would always feel like the man. During his time in D.C., I might have visited three times to hang out. But as time progressed, we went our separate ways and I stayed in New York to concentrate on my career.

Roughly a year later, I got an email from a friend highlighting an article that accused my radio friend of allegedly murdering two people. I was in shock, but not totally. I had not heard from him in more than a year and definitely was not about to contact him.

One night while hanging in Harlem, a guy approached me like he was scared and appeared to be shaking. He wanted to let me know that it was his friend that my radio friend allegedly murdered. I told him I knew nothing about his comment and kept it moving. I started to wonder how many more people would approach me on the matter, so I decided to limit my time in Harlem.

I was still working in independent radio promotions and it sustained my income temporarily. It wasn't helping me bring in what I was used to bringing in. However, I needed the check so I got my records played by any means necessary. I later found out that my old company, ABC, was looking for an agent again. Now that I had the experience under my belt,

I felt I could go back there and "win."

I had high hopes that things would be different and better since almost fifteen years had passed since I last worked there. The music and artists had changed so I expected them to at least have grown with the times. They hadn't. It was the same old shit, just a different year. I came in like a hungry lion trying to grab as many artists as I could. I signed Chaka Khan, Larry Graham, Dave Hollister, Eric Gabel, and a few others.

However, I was only able to stomach a year there. I had had enough again when I came to the realization that the company was still doing things in a primitive and outdated way. They didn't operate as a dynamic or innovative company, growing and changing with technology, society, or the world even. In order to stay current, a company must know how to evolve and ABC was just fine with being a dinosaur.

The last straw was when Oscar made the mistake of thinking he could still talk to me in a condescending way. By then, I had spent too much time in the streets so my mentality had changed. I didn't have to take it then, and I was definitely not taking it *now*. I quickly let Oscar know that although I wasn't in the streets, I knew how to "get street" if I needed to. So, I left the agency and took Dave Hollister with me and began managing him.

Dave was and still is a very talented brother. At the time we had different visions and after a year, we parted ways. Today, I am his booking agent, which just goes to show that sometimes, in relationships, it is truly all about timing.

## CHAPTER 35

# JAIL HOUSE ROCK

One night after work, I decided to visit a friend who had just moved to Washington Heights, a known drug area. When I got to his apartment, he wasn't there, so I got back in my car and proceeded to drive home. I was on 163rd Street in Harlem, when a van that was in front of me suddenly stopped. I started blowing my horn and decided to go around the van. All of a sudden, six guys jumped out of the van with their guns drawn. They each took positions around the car surrounding me. They were pointing guns in my face, on each side of the car, and at the back.

One guy on the driver's side yelled, "Put your hands on the steering wheel and do not move!" As I looked closely, I realized they were undercover police officers and they continued to give me commands.

"Get out of the car! Put your hands on the hood of the car! You got any drugs or weapons?" He yelled and I answered, "No." He grabbed my arms, cuffing me as the other officers began to search my vehicle.

Another officer asked if I was sure that I wasn't hiding

anything because if they found it, they were going to impound my car. I again told him I didn't have anything.

At that moment, I found myself in the back of the white paddy wagon that didn't have windows, with a few other people who were in handcuffs. The team of plainclothes officers were obviously doing a "sweep" and taking any prisoners they could. That's when one of the guys explained to me that because I was in that area with Jersey plates, I was a presumed drug dealer or there to buy drugs. It was very common for drug dealers to move right over the George Washington Bridge into Jersey and come back on a daily basis to still run their business.

I looked around the van and had an awful thought of ending up in the bullpen with these guys. My mind was racing because I then had an even scarier thought of them planting something in my car. *Damn!* I thought. I started thinking about my career, my wife, my life, and my job.

By the time they rounded up a group of us, it was about two hours later and I was on my way to jail to "The Tombs." I was commanded to strip and be searched. I couldn't fathom how I was even being booked, when there was not even anything in my car or on my person.

After being searched, I was then sat down at an officer's desk. I was in awe at the amount of cameras and surveillance that was in the area and what they could really see going on in the street. Plain as day I saw the "schedule" on a board of their procedure of running sweeps on Tuesdays and Thursdays.

One thing I learned for sure is I do not like being in

handcuffs. The feeling of not having freedom scared the shit out of me and sitting in that chair just made it worse.

My next stop was the bullpen. By the time I got in there, it was as crowded as a club, just without the presence of our female counterparts. I started talking to and befriended a guy that was in his 60s. I was about thirty-eight at the time. He seemed to be a pro at the process, an "in-house lawyer" having experienced this circumstance many times before. I told him how the whole scenario went down and he assured me that I would "be outta there in no time." For me it was too many minutes already.

As I sat there, I couldn't help but notice the presence of an open toilet. My nose knew of it moments before my eyes spotted it. There were no walls or doors around it and certainly no window by it to release the smells that were being produced. Just a nasty-looking and disgusting, stomach-turning, gross commode right in the corner with a line of men waiting. A line that looked like it was outside the club. People had that look like "I got to shit bad "on their faces.

There were a couple of chairs and only one bench. People were lined around the walls, standing or sitting on the dirty floor. As soon as there became room on the bench for me to sit, I did. No sooner than I sat and took a deep breath, I was surrounded again, but not by the police this time. There were two Hispanic men standing over me, telling me to get up out of their seats. When I refused, that number grew from two to four. I kindly got up and moved. At that moment, I realized I was in there with no friends, nobody to have my back, just me, myself and I. The thought of a beatdown became reality in my mind.

Someone started smoking weed and when the corrections officer asked who it was, he was pissed when no one answered him. I would imagine everyone, including me, was just trying to mind their own business and get out of there. No one was applying to be a police officer or do his job. He threatened that since no one spoke up, he would make it so that we would be last to get seen by the judge. **#3 Keep your mouth Shut.** He who knows don't tell and he who tells don't know.

Dinner time came around about ten. Crazy right? Well let's just say the mini box of Chocolate Cocoa Krispies with chocolate milk and an orange was not my idea of a wholesome meal or part of a dinner menu at all. People were throwing their oranges and boxes of cereal on the floor and I went into survival mode as if I were on the "Survivor" television series and gathered up some extra oranges just in case this horrible day turned into a disastrous week behind bars.

The lines for the phone were too long for me to try to use my complimentary phone call to call anyone. Bedtime was approaching as midnight was, too. I looked around and noticed my Gucci shoes getting a lot of attention. Still in survival mode, I decided not to become a robbery victim while sleeping. I wrapped my shoes in my coat and then put the whole thing under my head as a pillow.

The next morning, I was told that I was going to see the judge as I was moved to another cell. The cell was filled with only four other guys, but they all looked like they had done hard time. There was no telling if any of these guys had had a "body" on their "jacket" so I stayed to myself.

To my surprise, after about four hours in the cell, the officer called out my name. I was summoned for and released on my own, without even seeing the judge. I was also lectured when I asked why I had been made to stay so long if they knew I was not guilty. I was told that it was to teach me a lesson to stay out of that neighborhood.

I walked out and it was the next day. The feeling was as bad or as worse as walking out of "The Book" that morning. I wasn't high but I surely felt like I was in the twilight zone. I felt like a zombie stepping out of a cave in broad daylight.

That was the beginning of my participation in Tae Kwon Do, something I always wanted to do but now had more reason to go for it. I figured if that ever happened to me again, God forbid, at least I wouldn't have to get off the bench when challenged.

## CHAPTER 36

# FRIENDS

No sooner than I got out, I went right back into hustle mood. I was still trying to get back in the game, but the record industry was like musical chairs. Once you were out, it was almost impossible to get back in unless you had friends that would look out for you. That's when I realized the difference between friends and "industry friends." Whodini defines it in this way:

> *"Friends is a word we use every day.*
> *Most the time we use it in the wrong way.*
> *Now you can look the word up, again and again.*
> *But the dictionary doesn't know the meaning of friends."*

I realized I was on my own and no one was coming with a check or a job so I needed to do what I could to keep myself moving. I didn't want to lose my house so I did what I had to do.

One day I went to do some office work for a friend at Brunswick Records. While we were meeting, he asked if I knew anyone who would put posters around the city and I told him I would let him know. After seeing the budget, I decided to just do it myself.

This was work that had to be done before the crack of dawn, about three in the morning, before most people get up for work. I started posting bills in Manhattan and quickly learned that it was not a one-man job. At all. I went to Harlem to enlist some people who would be looking for any kind of money and any kind of work. I paid two gentlemen, who appeared to delight in the "pipe," one dollar per poster. They worked really hard and diligently until their pay had accumulated to twenty bucks. That's when they decided to retire after reaching their goal of $20. They quit on me, so I lowered my price to fifty cents per poster and employed two new gentlemen. My two replacements had to be fired because I caught them smacking posters up any which way just so they could scrounge up enough in pay up to "beam them up to Scotty" like the other two. They were done after making ten dollars.

As I was returning back downtown, I noticed that some of my posters had already been taken down and even drove past a guy in the process of taking one down. I stopped to question him, and he explained that you can't just put posters up anywhere for any event. "WE CONTROL THE MARKET." It was almost as bad as the mafia controlling the ports. Like there were people who basically had areas on "lock" and expected payment just to be able to display anything in their zone. I'd be damned if I was going to be muscled over some posters, so I returned to Harlem.

This epic fail led me to rethink and resort back to the promotional people I knew. I went to talk to an OG in the game named Max, who was an independent promotions guy, and figured he may have something for me. I might add that Max was also a drug supplier. Due to him being my neighbor, I had run errands or helped him with fixing house matters before, so I wasn't a stranger to him. Things got a little hairy with him because on two separate occasions, he had done deliveries with me in the car and I didn't like that. Then, on another occasion, we met some Columbians in FT Lee, NJ. They arrived in a limo on Jones Road in just enough time to make the transaction and head back to the city. To me, that was too obvious and too risky. I wasn't willing to risk my freedom just because I had decided to ride with someone who wanted to play Dr. Feelgood. After having experienced many other close encounters, "riding dirty" was just not something that I was not willing or interested in doing.

## CHAPTER 37

# CHIEF ROCKER

One night, Max asked me to come and fix a CD player. After I arrived, he began to entertain his company. His doorbell sounded but he was in the other room so I answered the door. When I opened the door, I was shocked at who was standing in front of me. It was none other than Frankie Crocker of WBLS. He greeted me cordially and I went and got Max from the other room.

They had a short conversation before Frankie went into a room by himself while Max went and continued to entertain his company. I was curious to know why he went into a room by himself. I played it off by knocking and asking if he wanted anything. Surprisingly, he was in the room reading The Bible. I went to get him some water at his request and was puzzled as to why there was partying going on in one room and Bible study in the other. When I brought him the glass of water, I asked what he was reading, and he acted as though he did not hear me at first (I guess he wanted to finish reading) and then he shared a verse with me. Just as he was about to elaborate on the scripture, I was summoned to the "party room."

I ended up getting stuck in a conversation and missed my opportunity for an exchange with Mr. Crocker that probably would have been meaningful for me to this day. I always wondered what he would have said had I left the "OGs" alone and gone back. It bothered me after his death (I am not sure of how much time passed before it) that he may have been dealing with something so serious and that I didn't pull myself back to spend that quality time with him. I didn't know he was sick, and it still bothers me that I never finished that conversation. R. I. P. Frankie.

* * *

I got a call from Keith Ingram, a friend of mine who wanted me to meet with a lawyer named Londell McMillan. I had met Londell years prior, when he had first graduated from law school. Londell was now a powerful attorney who represented Chaka Khan, Ruff Riders, some of Murder Ink's artists, Michael Jackson, Prince, and many others.

During a meeting, he shared that Prince wanted to start his own distribution company. After having worked in so many parts of the music industry, this was right up my alley. I knew I was the right man for the job. We spent weeks establishing the blueprint for the company and what was going to be needed for it to be successful.

Weeks after our meeting, Prince requested to meet with the team, which included me and a college frat brother of mine, Rudy Smith, who was also a lawyer. Prince flew us out first class. I cannot disclose what transpired in the meeting. However, I will say that after our meeting, he showed me all of the performance rooms at Paisley Park. There was the jazz room, concert hall, the area room, which looked like a big supermarket, and a very small cafe room. He had recently changed his name so like many, I didn't know what to call him. I just called him Sir. After the meeting, we went to have lunch and I was surprised that it was just a salad, a lot of healthy vegetables, and beans. There was only pure juice and water. No fried chicken, greens, and potato salad. Lol. After we ate, we were whisked back to the airport to return home. We spent three hours on the flight there and two and a half hours for the meeting. We were on the flight longer than we were meeting.

# CHAPTER 38

# THROUGH THE FIRE

As things developed within the company, I began to spend a lot of time with Chaka Khan and Larry Graham, developing their labels and distribution under Prince's company. While I was on the road with Larry, I asked what do you call Sir? He shared that he called Prince "Baby Brother." I just continued to call him "Sir."

Larry and I became very close. So, when he asked me for my address one day, and then later when the Jehovah Witnesses came knocking on my door, I felt I knew exactly how they found me because it was Larry's religion.

One night during one of Prince's impromptu concerts, he decided to do a show at a small club called Tramps in Manhattan on 21ˢᵗ Street. The concert had just started when I was approached by a security guard outside who said there was someone who wanted to see me. When I walked outside, I immediately recognized both people standing in front of me. The gentleman walked up and said, "Hi, my name is Benny Medina and this is my new artist, Jennifer Lopez." Before he could state his business, I said, "Benny I know who you are.

We worked in the record business together." Then I let Jennifer know I was aware of her and her new single. They seemed at ease and then they requested tickets to see Prince. Without hesitation, I brought both of them in and sat them up front. I say all this to say that I'm still waiting to see Jennifer now that she has blown up.

One of my jobs with Prince was to set up the after-parties for the shows. These were the parties for guests and celebrities. I remember seeing Eddie Murphy's name on the guest list one night. I was excited and couldn't wait to see him again. It had been about ten years since I had been in his presence.

When he arrived, I saw him at the door and I walked up to greet him. I said hello and waited for a happy greeting, but

*Larry Graham & Mark Green*

nothing happened. He said, "Hi." I definitely expected a warmer greeting. I felt honored to be in his presence and figured he would have at least acknowledged my presence as well, since I worked for him at one time. When I realized he didn't receive me the same way I had greeted him, I reminded him of who I was. "Eddie, it's me, Mark Green," to which he said, "I know who you are" and continued to display a stone face.

On that note, I did not know how to respond so I continued to move forward as if he was a VIP I didn't know. I sat him and his guest at the table and said if there is anything else you need, please let me know.

What I have learned in this business is you can't take these things personally. However, it took me a long time to realize and digest these types of actions. There are at least four actors that have invited me to their homes and parties

*Chaka Khan & Mark Green*

but when I call them to tell them I have work for them or some type of financial employment, it takes them forever to call back or sometimes they don't call at all.

Humility is attractive but it was just another lesson learned. Just because you are doing business with someone, it doesn't mean they're your friend. You must continue to remind yourself that no matter what you face, *the show must go on!* Whether you are in the entertainment business or not. In life you must keep pushing, no matter what.

We continued to tour promoting Larry's and Chaka's albums. Although the main focus was Prince's "1999" re-release. I thought it would be a great idea to go back to Tru Tone to have them press up the record in an expedited manner. Since I already had a relationship with them, I figured I would get a more reasonable price. Unfortunately, the lady in charge was not impressed because she wasn't even aware of who Prince was. Unbelievable.

I wanted to press one hundred and fifty thousand records which should have made her enthusiastic. She could have made a lot of money but instead she showed her true colors by telling me, with no shame, "Well can I speak to the people in charge because I know you know how to jive with the brothers." In shock, I retorted with a subtle yet smarter remark. "I know how to jive with the white folk, too."

She was a bit taken aback and her face turned red as an apple but probably didn't figure that her words were "parting words" for me until I never came around to do business with them again. It was things like that that made me angry and although sometimes I had to grin and bear it, I also knew how to give someone back the same negative energy they were giving me. So, I gave the project to her competitor.

## CHAPTER 39

# STRICTLY BUSINESS

I spent a lot of time with the artists while making sure that Larry Graham, Chaka Khan, and Prince's music was distributed properly. I was in charge of distribution and one problem was that some companies would buy in bulk and then try to re-distribute the copies to make more of a profit than us by upselling it.

One day I walked into the office and was greeted by my old boss, Danny, who'd fired me from EMI. I was shocked to see him, and at the same time, the thought of beating his ass came to mind. Londell reintroduced us and said he would be assisting us with the company. I was not happy

*Juvenile & Mark Green*

at all. I made sure to let Londell know that I was not taking any orders from this dude. He agreed and things began to move smoothly. I kept my eye on "ole boy" and I made sure he knew I was running the project. He stayed in his lane and I never had any problems from him.

Over time, Prince realized that self-distribution was very costly and risky. When you are under a major label, they do all the work. He decided to dissolve his company and sign with Arista Records for a year while he mapped out his next move.

I also began to map out my next move as this was the story of my life. I always found the "next thing" or it always found me. A couple of my friends who were agents reached out to see if I was interested in starting a booking agency. I said I was and that I could contribute $10,000 to form the company.

By the time we were to set up the company, they no longer wanted my money but just wanted to use my services and expertise as an employee. I took the job as a booking agent, making a salary of $75,000. As the company began to develop, the "Dirty South" was making waves and an impact on Hip-Hop. There wasn't much going on for them up North, but they were definitely blowing up in their neck of the woods.

I started booking for Lil John & the East Side Boyz. They were a group from Atlanta. Another new up-and-coming artist from Atlanta that I was booking was T.I. Then Memphis had a duo named 8 Ball and MJG. Then New Orleans bred a rapper named Juvenile that I was working with, too. These artists were putting the South on the map.

After about a year with American Talent, I decided to break out and start my own booking agency. Working with that agency gave me the experience that I needed to spread my wings and fly to my own coop. It was long after I moved that

I received a call from a college friend, Rob Mason, who needed a place to stay temporarily. He was going through some personal issues at the time.

Rob came up from Atlanta and about two weeks after he arrived, I received a phone call from a promoter by the name of Steve Branch. Steve wanted to book Freddie Jackson, Morris Day, Keith Sweat, and the Gap Band. At the time, my company wasn't off the ground yet. I was in the process of incorporating it, so when I got the call, I said ok, but I immediately went into panic mode. Here was a chance for me to make $10,000 but the only drawback was my lack of being computer savvy.

Rob had already started working on his business and decided to help me get started. I created a company name and logo to get the deal done, before someone else came in and grabbed it. He helped me leverage a computer and I learned the rest along the way. I had to have files, Excel sheets, financial records, and reports. I had always basically worked for some other company that had a pre-built infrastructure. Now I needed to go into "Boss Mode."

*Mark Green & Rob Mason*

I took my money and bought two desks, two phones, and two computers. Now I had to train and employ someone. Rob was that person.

Rob didn't quite understand the business, so he got off to a slow start. I knew what I knew because I did what I did. He had never done any of this before. I explained that his job was to be on the phones, shopping artists, and although it seemed simple to me, it wasn't as easy for him. He would rather sleep. You would have thought he was actually outside beating the pavement. He would work for a while and then have to take a nap. That would annoy me. I was perturbed. I knew how to make deals, book shows, and he was acting like it was rocket science.

One day, I overheard him on the phone, and it was unbelievable to me that he was actually mixing up numbers and was oblivious to it. I had to reiterate the game to him but knowing that he could cause me to lose money, I had to start monitoring him more. I surely didn't have the time or patience to babysit anyone. If I did, I wouldn't have needed him to work for me in the first place. He didn't have the passion for it and he was unfulfilled by it and bored. I was excited about my vast career. To him it was a job and a job that he didn't love.

After a while, I gradually let him off the hook. Eventually it was just time to send him back from whence he came. Rob has always been a great friend and a big supporter. I owe a lot to him for helping me start my company, and he will always have a special place in my heart. In the end, I think we helped each other accomplish our goals and now we can look back and be proud of where we stand.

## CHAPTER 40

# SOUND OF DA POLICE

L ooking back on it, I have come to realize that what I do is a skill. I have a talent. I know how to formulate relationships over the phone, give people what they want, and get what I want at the same time.

During this time, I ran into my friend Kim McClow, who introduced me to a guy named Kenny Tinsley. Kenny and I hit it off right from the intro. We began to hang out daily and we had a lot in common. We both knew each other's names from our high school days but had never met. Kenny and I graduated around the same time and both of us went to HBCUs. Unfortunately, he pledged Kappa Alpha Psi (lol) and I pledged the greatest fraternity in the world, Omega Psi Phi. Kenny would go on to be one of my best friends and we kept each other grounded and focused on our goals. Kenny was a saving grace for me and led me out of the destructive life that I was leading. Even though I would sometimes times put him in compromising situations, he always found a way to get out and pull me out with him. Our story alone could be another book, but for now, I just say thank you, Kenny, for your friendship.

Things actually began looking up. Business was taking off and I started exclusively dating one woman in particular. Her name was Carmen and we also met through my long-time friend Kim, who introduced me to Kenny. After dating for a while, Carmen suggested I move in with her and use the money I was paying rent with to open an office. I was a little reluctant at first, but I decided to give it a shot. As the company progressed, so did our relationship.

While in the process of moving, I had furniture that I needed to get rid of. I ran into a guy I knew named Jay Green (no relation). I was already apprehensive about giving up my freedom, now I was giving up my furniture. It made it seem so final. I learned a hard lesson.

I gave Jay my furniture and he gave me an IOU. He was supposed to pay me for it later. When later never came, I went to his house calling out his name. When he came outside, he was unapologetic about not keeping his word, so we got into a fight. I managed to grab up his "little black book" thinking it would be worth it to him to get it back. He wanted it back, alright. He wanted it back so bad that he called the cops on me. I ended up having to fight a charge of grand larceny because he claimed the book was more than $250.

It took me some time to clear my name. Unluckily for us, our last names were the same. So, the judge got confused about who was who and also disgusted about the whole "petty ordeal" that the whole case was thrown out and we each had to pay a $200 fine. It didn't end there, though. I still had to fight to get that charge off my record.

Hell, I was riding through Hackensack when I got pulled over by police for some bogus stop. As he began to ask me questions, he asked had I ever been arrested, and I said no. That's when he told me I still had a charge on my record. I had to go back to court, which took about three months to have that expunged from my record. For once, me being stopped by the police paid off.

Listen, I can't make this stuff up. That's why I am here to share my stories because there has never been a dull moment. But as usual, you know the rest—***the show must go on!***

As I stated earlier, I was working with some of the new artists from the South, and things were going great. I took them and began to really focus on helping them make a name for themselves up North.

I was then making six figures and I needed more employees. I hired a girl from around the way named Sheila Wade and she was a people person with the gift of gab. She was personable, funny, and entertaining. She was able to get what we wanted in the most charming way. After establishing Sheila and being able to leave her to get things done, I continued with my other endeavors in the music industry.

One day I got a call from the same independent promoter friend who wanted me to work a couple of records for him. During a project I was working, I ran into Aaliyah. I was wowed by her. She had such an aura and presence that I was eager to work with her. Just looking at her, you could see the beauty and feel the kindness of this princess. She was an angel.

There was something about her that drew any and everyone to her. We started talking about the past tour we were on together and she made mention about going back on

*Mark Green & Aaliyah*

tour. I requested to be on that tour, and she liked the idea. We had planned on talking in the next few days about my position and duties after she spoke to her manager. Unfortunately, it never happened due to the plane crash that took her life. RIP Baby girl, you were truly Heaven sent.

I was devastated about the news and it took me a long time to get over it. The fact that she was so young and had so much promise was disturbing. I decided to attend the funeral and it was just so sad to see her body come down the street in that glass carriage. I had been around death so many times for all the wrong reasons that it constantly reminded me to get my life in order.

# CHAPTER 41

# JUST TO GET A REP

I started looking back over my life and reminiscing about all the crazy encounters I had put myself in, flashing back to the late 80s. Things like buying drugs for clients. I was always questioned about being a police officer because my attire did not look like I was from the streets. I never allowed my appearance to fall off, and I always kept myself up.

The year was 1999 and Jay Z, Method Man, Redman, and DMX's "Hard Knock Life" Tour was complete and had done

**HARD KNOCK LIFE TOUR**

Featuring Jay-Z, DMX, Method Man, and Redman

As of February 19, 19

| | CITY | VENUE | CAPACITY | PROMOTER CONTACT | RADIO STATION/PD | COMMENT |
|---|---|---|---|---|---|---|
| ay 27 | Charlotte | Charlotte Coliseum 100 Paul Buck Blvd. Charlotte, NC 28217 (704) 357-4101 | 15,000 | Randy Bazzell (502) 946-7280 | WPEG/Andre Carson (704) 333-0131 | • Wants Jan 99 • Meet & Greet cookies • Tix in process • On broadcast • Winning on Cool |
| ay 28 | Charleston, SC | Charleston Coliseum 5001 Coliseum Drive N Charleston, SC 29418 (809) 529-5050 | 11,000 | Gino Narratil Victoria Entertainment (757) 497-8180 | WWWZ/Terry Base (843) 308-9300 WPAL/Jet Jackson (843) 763-6330 | • Exclusive show • Meet & Greet cookies • Without promos • Two-paid running |
| 2 | Washington DC | MCI Center 601 F Street NW Washington DC (202) 628-3200 | 14,500 | Cellar Door Brian O Connell (703) 643-1900 | WPGC/Jay Stevens (301) 441-3500 | • Exclusive Show • Official Tour video feed • Tweens, Giveaways, & T • Roving Chances • Tix giveaway • Tix on sale 3/10 • In Promo Spot • Meet & Greet cookies |
| 3 | East Rutherford | Continental Airlines Arena 50 State Highway 120 East Rutherford, NJ (201) 935-3900 | 12,600 | Metropolitan Carl Freed (573) 744-0770 | HOT 97/Tracy Cloherty (212) 367-1661 | • Star City taping breaks • Exclusive Show • Big City taping blocks • Break out • Tix on sale 1/22 • Meet & Greet cookies • Tour Spot running |
| 4 | Cleveland | CSU Convocation Ce 2000 Prospect Avenue (216) 687-5454 | 10,250 | Michael Belkin (440) 247-2722 | WZAK/Bobby Rush (216) 521-9300 | • Tix giveaway |

very well. People were surprised at the outcome. For some reason, everyone thought the first major Hip-Hop tour was going to be troublesome and deadly. But to everyone's surprise, it was a major success. No sooner than the drop of the ball in 2000, it seemed as though every major booking agency was on a mission to sign a Hip-Hop artist.

That tour made so much money that before I knew it, they were offering movie deals, commercials, and TV shows to all the artists. All the main artists I had signed were leaving my agency like we had the plague. There was nothing I could do to compete with CAA, ICM, and William Morris. I lost T.I., Lil John, and Ludacris all with the stroke of a pen.

Then there was the takeover by Universal Attractions. They started going after all the acts I had and promising them a better situation if they signed with them. Although I was fighting and standing my ground, I was still making money but wasn't as lucrative as before.

Then in 2001, Carmen and I got married and things were great. I had a club I was running on the side and promoting shows and happy hours there. My business was steady and my employee, Sheila, was beginning to do very well. I was happy.

Then I got a call from a college friend, Jackie, who was working for a major liquor company. Jackie had made a name for herself in the Spirits industry and received a promotion to come to New York to head up the company. She called me to let me know she needed to book a jazz series that would promote one of her liquor brands. I was all in and reached out to one of my clients named Randy to help secure the club and some acts. Randy, on the other hand, called Barry, who used to work for a jazz station, to join in.

*Jacquie Lee & Mark Green*

I was a little apprehensive about this move because I felt I was losing control of what I had. These guys were trying to make moves with my money and tell me what they were going to pay me. I was not having it, but Jackie wanted to keep things as they were because she needed to justify her payment. I did not want to screw Jackie, so I played ball and accepted my position.

The concert series began to take off, and Jackie looked like a superstar, but behind the scenes, it got messy. The money was coming up short and there were too many cooks in the kitchen. I could not stand by any longer, so I put on my street clothes and my thug mentality and stepped to them to inform them that I would be handling the finances from that point on. Just as I started to get control, I ran into another situation.

The woman that owned the club was having financial problems. So while these guys were trying to get me, they were being got by the venue owner. She was using the money that she was supposed to pay them to keep her club open. I was fighting with three individuals. I was still making my money off the bookings, but I needed my percentage from the shows.

In the end, they were so busy trying to rip me off that they all lost. When the lady who owned the club could not deliver any money to anyone, I was the only one to come out on top because I got paid from the artists and I still got a percentage of the gross fees. By the time they went to collect from her, she had no more money.

## CHAPTER 42

# THE MESSAGE

Time passed, and 2003 came and with it, I received a call from none other than Grandmaster Flash. He said, "Mr. Green, I would like to talk to you about doing management."

At the time he was being managed by Lady Blue, who had managed him for years. But after an issue they had, he wanted to regroup and start fresh with someone else. After meeting with him and discussing the opportunity, I took him on as his manager. I liked how he presented himself and he was very humble and respectful.

As I began to try to book him, I was running into a lot of dead ends. He wasn't as easy to book in the United States, as I assumed he would be. Although he is truly a bonafide legend in Hip-Hop, his past seemed to catch up to him. I had to sit down and redirect his path to remarket him.

One good thing that came to light was how extremely popular he was overseas. He had a huge following in Europe. Actually, DJs are revered there and treated how we treat our performers here. I was in awe of the magnitude of the audience in the shows he was able to book. It was hard to fathom that a DJ was headlining a tour. In this country, that is unheard of. Even more shocking was the fact that Flash was hired to play for Queen Elizabeth II.

I looked into creating a show for him. We raised his performance fees and focused our attention on the UK, with great returns. After about two years, we parted ways, only for him to request that I return to manage him two more times.

Hip-Hop had transformed the music industry, from being the "forbidden fruit" or stepchild of "real" music, to becoming the catalyst for many things in media. Many artists were in high demand to sell commercial products. Hip-Hop changed the way we did business in the music industry.

It started to change the offerings of the contracts to multi-million-dollar deals. Artists began to ask for more money, and they were given what they wanted. In bookings, things also changed from an agent holding a deposit in escrow until after the performance, to turning the money right over to the artist, because of their power to pick and choose. This put a strain on an agent because the agent would be responsible for paying an artist up front so if the artist was a no-show, the promoter would be expecting the money to be returned from the booking agent.

The artists were becoming just as demanding, if not more demanding, than actors when it came to their riders and they were making outlandish requests for things to be given to them out of the promoters' pockets.

The face of the managers also changed from experienced

and professional people who worked for management companies, to aunts, uncles, friends, and cousins. Even local street thugs were in on the game. Everyone became a manager but not everyone had a clue about management. This made things very difficult for agents because we had to not only watch the money, but oftentimes, we had to start watching our backs because if we didn't accommodate the crazy ideas of the entourage, we could wind up looking for a place to hide out.

## CHAPTER 43

# CODE OF THE STREET

In 2004, I was approached by Guru of Gang Starr, for management. We had a long history dating back to when I was the Director of Promotions and then later I was booking their shows. They were managed by Fat Gary, who was also a friend of mine and who graciously gave me his blessings to manage his former artist. Things were going great. We were making a lot of money and doing a lot of shows overseas. Guru was hard working and focused on his craft.

Things suddenly changed after he left Premier and started working with a new producer and road manager named Sunny. I was perplexed because Guru seemed to be entranced by this new producer. He was giving this guy so much credit and I just didn't see the greatness that Guru tried to portray. I didn't understand why he gave the guy so many accolades. Guru was respected and had accomplished so many things with Premier before Sunny came along, that I didn't see what Sunny was bringing to the table that would make what was already a lucrative and successful endeavor, more prosperous.

What I did notice was a change in Guru's personality. His

self-esteem seemed to diminish. It was like he was losing his mojo. I couldn't put my finger on what was happening to him, I just knew he wasn't the same confident leader that he used to be.

As time went on, he started losing himself and control of his own destiny. Sunny was beginning to have control over any and everything that had to do with Guru's business. Sunny and I were at odds, and we had many contentious arguments. It was like watching a person you care about go down a dark path, but you can't stop them.

I was being pushed out of my duties, responsibilities, and rights as a manager. Although I expressed concern, Guru seemed fearful of Sunny. It was almost like he had some type of hold over him or maybe he had something on Guru that I didn't know. At any rate, it was bad. His whole aura was off.

One day, I booked them for an MTV event in London. After researching the promoter, I told Guru that the promoter had a bad reputation and he should make sure he got his money up front, before his performance. This was nothing new to artists because this was the standard they had set.

After the show was over, I immediately called Guru to find out how everything went. I asked if he had gotten paid. His response was that the guy had agreed to wire him the money later. I blacked out on Guru because I had warned him about this possibly happening. He assured me that the person was going to keep his word, but it just didn't make sense.

"Are you fucking serious?" I asked. "I told you to get your money because how are you going to get your money once you leave Europe and return to the United States? What is going to make him pay you, knowing that you can't easily get back to the UK, to make him give it to you? You would have already performed!"

Guru brushed it off until later never came and he never got his payment. Then, of course, he wanted to make me responsible for tracking this guy down to get what was owed to him. I emphatically refused to assist him because I clearly told him what to do, and he chose to do the total opposite.

As I was looking into the event, I discovered that Sunny had booked him for another two shows while they were there behind my back so they wouldn't have to give me my cut. As the days turned into weeks, Sunny began to call me and threaten me to get "his" money. There were many threats

*Guru & Mark Green*

swirling back and forth between the both of us and I was not backing down. It got so ugly that we began to even threaten each other's families.

Sunny and Guru showed up at my office days later and threatened my staff. They were so scared, they called the police and when they called me, I was furious. The first thing I did was take my guns out of the safety boxes and dust them off. I had to be ready for any showdown that they tried to bring so I had one gat in my car and kept another on me.

The police department called me, stating that they had reached out to Guru. He arrogantly asked them if they knew who he was. They informed him that they didn't care who he was and that if he came back into their jurisdiction, he would be arrested.

Although I was ready for war, I was also perturbed at the fact that I had to watch my back, including circling my house every time I arrived to make sure no one was hiding in wait for me. It was sad and it was a shame because Sunny had ruined what had been a great business/friendly relationship. But it was either going to be them or me and it wasn't going to be me.

The threats got so intense that I was ready to just handle what I had to handle and get it over with. It had gotten so bad that I was receiving phone calls at home in the middle of the night with my wife there. I figured, why be a sitting duck and let them catch me with my pants down? They knew where I lived. It was time to take it to the streets.

I knew I could handle it in the streets, but the better side of my brain convinced me not to end up in jail. So, I had to rely on my business savvy to win. They say to work smarter and not harder. Neither one of them were worth losing everything I had worked so hard for. The light bulb went off in my head, and I thought up a plan to hit him where it would really hurt—his pockets.

I called Guru and asked, "How are you going to explain to the IRS that you had more than $20,000 in cash that you never reported to them?" I figured out that the reason he didn't want to receive the money from the MTV guy and had agreed to have it wired to him was because of those two other shows that they booked without my knowledge. They had that cash and would have to explain it at customs when they returned to the U.S. and of course, that would mean having to pay taxes on that money. He thought he was slick by telling the other guy to wire it to him once he returned. He didn't want to do that and he also would not want to have to be taxed or even receive penalties or possibly receive jail time. With that call, the beef was squashed. I still laugh about it all the time. All this gangster shit, and these two folded like a stack of cards with the mention of three letters—IRS. Who would have thought that three little letters could end a war? I never heard from either one of them again regarding that money. Period, end of story. **Rule#5.C.R.E.A.M**

Like many other times before, I had to hear of his passing, and it made me feel bad that he died so young. I feel bad about how his life ended. He was such a great artist and a joy to work with and I have so many good memories that I did not share. I cherish the good times we had and will hold on to those until we meet again. R.I.P. Guru.

## CHAPTER 44

# WHAT'S MY NAME?

What people don't understand about this business is that all that glitters ain't gold. Everything that looks good with the glitz and glamor has a lot of tarnished spots that people do not see. I love what I do and I wouldn't trade it or my experiences for the world, but I am writing this book to tell my story, from my side. I cannot take credit for the artists who are extremely talented but I also want to leave my mark and my legacy. People in entertainment brighten up our rainy days and give us therapy. I would like to think that some of the great shows I have been involved in producing have given people joy and unforgettable moments. And I am very proud of it. I could have been killed many times. I could have thrown in the towel and every time I thought about doing something else, I would get the right phone call to confirm that this is my calling. But as we say in my business, no matter the circumstances, *the show must go on!*

On that note, I had booked DMX for a show in Chile and everything was going as planned. Then, the day before the show, he didn't show up. He had already gotten half of his money up front and he was a no-show in Chile but not in Miami where he was on TV. He may have ghosted them initially but him being broadcast live led the Chile promoters right to him. They had been calling me and looking for answers but thank God for that live broadcast. Yep. They came to the U.S. and got him and escorted him overseas where he was supposed to be. Dealing with DMX was definitely an adventure. On another occasion, while working for the law firm that represented DMX, I was asked to go on the road as the road manager for DMX & The Lox for a particular event in Charlotte, NC. His uncle Ray was the manager and we hit it off just right. However, as soon as we landed and went by the venue, Ray and I were escorted into a room and held up by four angry muscle-bound thugs that demanded some money that was owed to them. I had no idea what was going on. They said we were not leaving that room until we dished up the funds. I was clueless, so they put us in different rooms and grilled us. After a while, they realized I had nothing to do with the past engagement and let me go. I don't know what happened to Ray but he eventually came out unscathed. There was never a dull moment with X. RIP DMX. Long live my dawg!

The Lox, on the other hand, did not want me. They cashed me in like a lottery ticket and kept it moving. I was cool with it because they were a handful anyway.

## Chapter 45

# FLASH TO THE BEAT

At the same time, I got another call from Grandmaster Flash. This was the second time he requested me to manage him. We started spending a lot of time in the UK. I had already been to about ten countries and saw traveling as a great experience. I had been talking to Flash for about two years about writing a book. I didn't know anything about publishing a book, I just knew he had a great story. I had been reading a lot of biographies by an author named David Ritz who had written a few other successful biographies from other artists. He had written Marvin Gaye's book, Aretha, Gladys, Elvis, BB King, and Smokey

Robinson's life stories, to name a few.

The first thing I did was ask Google how to publish a

book. I also reached out to a number of book publishers to see what the procedure would be for them to finance and promote a novel about a famous DJ who was one of the living legends of Hip-Hop, who had been influential in the birth of the genre.

I contacted one of my friends, Chrisena Coleman, who agreed to write the treatment for the book. She was an author who had a good following. She wrote *Just About Girlfriends*, *Mama Knows Best* and *Global Grind*, to name a few. After I received the treatment, I decided to hit the pavement to shop the book for a book deal. I went to Simon & Schuster, Regan Books, William Morris, and finally landed the deal with Doubleday. It only took a couple of weeks because I was able to convince the lady that Flash was known all over the word for inventing a type of mixing of two songs together while playing them both simultaneously and moving from one song to the next while implementing something called, "The quick mix theory." I knew the book would be a hit. She took my word for it and I was elated, but she wasn't sure about Chrisena being the one to pen it. I immediately thought of David Ritz and unbeknownst to me, he was one of Doubleday's writers. So, the show was about to go down! The book is titled, *The Adventures of Grandmaster Flash!*

I was optimistic about the idea of him doing book signings and book tours, etc. He did not want to put in the work to do interviews and TV shows. Tension began to build between us. I knew it wouldn't be long before he would *again* fire me. About six months after the book was released, he let me go.

I saw it as my release to another endeavor. I had been down that road before and wasn't too surprised. All good things must come to an end, even not-so-great things and everything in between. Change in life is inevitable but he actually replaced me with a woman named Miss Parker, and the saga continued.

# CHAPTER 46

# R.E.S.P.E.C.T

Although there are always new artists, one thing that is not always consistent is the money. You can make a hundred thousand dollars one year and feel like you need to be on the soup line the next. My money started acting funny because this business is about sales and like I said before, the major artists were leaving to join ranks with the major agencies, and that meant splitting my money more ways. Sometimes, you would have to do a buy and sell. I would buy at a low price and then sell it at a higher price to make a profit. My position is truly that of a hustler.

One day I read an article about a concert hall that was reopening in my neighborhood. I decided to go and speak to someone to introduce myself and let them know I could bring some great acts there. While speaking to the director, I realized she had just started and seemed to be on her own and unaware of what really goes into producing events. She gave me a shot to be included in the building of the venue and it was on and poppin' after that.

I started booking a lot of urban artists like Al Green,

Chaka Khan, and Teena Marie, to name a few. Being from the neighborhood allowed me to have more control than I thought I would and it was great because I was also able to hire people that I knew. Within two months, I moved up the ranks and became the general manager. I basically had carte blanche to bring my ideas and as long as I could keep the people buying tickets and attending the shows, I was in a great position. I always learned a lesson from the things that transpired, so my takeaway from this moment in my life was not to hire people that you know. Nepotism is a no-no. *(Rule #9: **Keep Family and Friends Separate from Your Business**)*

I was hiring people I trusted but instead, I got people that flipped on me. I had to fire three of my friends, and although we are still friends, it was an uncomfortable dilemma I didn't feel responsible for. While I had their backs, they were stabbing me in mine. One thing I learned in business is that friendship and business do not mix. It's like oil and water.

I'd been at the theater for a few years and things were great. Sheila was running my business, and I was running the Bergen Performing Arts Center. By this time, my daughter was in high school and had started spending more time with me. When Janay was very young, she had a knack for words. I remember riding down the street and she asked me how to spell "Mick" and then she said how do you spell Donald? I think she was in second grade. Before I could answer, I saw McDonalds. It did not take long before she was admitted to the Governor's school in Petersburg, V.A. It was a school for gifted and talented students. It was there that she discovered her desire to speak Spanish.

I wanted to get Janay involved in the theater but she wasn't interested in it. She had her own ideas. She was gifted in the arts and loved Spanish culture, as I did when I was young. She actually started a Spanish Club in high school and received a full scholarship to four Ivy League colleges. Janay decided to accept the academic scholarship from a private college in Virginia. We weren't able to spend that much time together so we decided that she would stay with me for the summers.

To my surprise, I was given the opportunity to take over the programming at Bergen Performing Arts Center when my boss was terminated. This was exciting for me because in the past, the majority of the events were cultural events and every now and then, there'd be a Motown artist but that was the extent of how performing arts theaters were programmed. Now, I was about to bring in all of the artists I'd grown up on. I wanted to bring in performers who had never really played at performing arts theaters. So, I booked groups like Foreigner, Styxx, Chicago, Al Green, Lou Rawls, and the list goes on. Things were going so well that they extended my budget, which allowed me to book Earth, Wind & Fire, Dianna Ross, and Aretha Franklin. Before I knew it, I became the man in the town. Wherever I would go, people would offer me free food, free drinks, free entry to clubs, etc.

I soon had the confidence and the backing of the chairman to continue to bring in superstars. We only had 1,300 seats, and some of the artists were demanding up to six figures, which made it almost impossible to book them. But I also had some great relationships that allowed me to negotiate lower fees. One of those relationships was with Aretha Franklin's agent. After our brief discussion, he agreed to give me Aretha.

The morning of her show, I received a call from her agent wanting to make sure that we would be paying the balance to Ms. Franklin in cash. I had to inform the agent that we are a non-profit theater and cannot pay performers in cash as that is not normal business procedure for performing arts theaters. We called the chairman and expressed her request to him and he advised me to contact the bookkeeper. The bookkeeper was directed to set up the transaction at the bank, and to have Ms. Franklin's money prepared. He made a call to Aretha and informed her that we would give her a check to endorse and then cash it for her so that there would be a paper trail.

I made arrangements to meet Aretha at the Ritz Hotel where she frequently stayed when in New York. When I arrived at her room, her manager answered the door and escorted me to her "parlor" where I was greeted by her, in her nightgown.

After a small reintroduction, I presented her the check for her to sign. She looked at me and said, "Where is the money?"

I told her that her agent was aware that we were going to bring the check for her to sign and that she would get her money at the show. She said she wasn't going to sign the check without the money. She walked away and went back into her room.

When I got back to Jersey, I was angry and embarrassed. I thought things were already taken care of and everyone understood what was happening. I asked the bookkeeper to meet me at the bank. We went to the bank, and the teller handed over seventy-five thousand dollars in cash and gave us a private room to count the funds. Neither the bookkeeper nor I wanted to take the time to count all of the money. How would a bank not give the right amount? We returned to the office and placed the money in the safe that was safeguarded by both of us having to use our keys to retrieve the money.

Before Aretha was to come, I was informed that she had to have a hot dressing room and to make sure there was no AC on in the theater. So, I went to her dressing room early that morning and I put two heaters in the room, had all of the lights on to make sure that the room was roasting like an oven. When Aretha arrived, I immediately contacted the bookkeeper to come to the safe so we could take out the money. We took the money out, and the bookkeeper went back to her office, and I went to meet with Ms. Franklin to give her the money for the show. As soon as I put the stacks in her hand, she started counting them.

*Aretha Franklin & Mark Green*

By the time she got through the first half of the money, she was sweating bullets and fanning herself. By the time she counted the third stack she was complaining that the room was too hot and told me to "Open that door!" I was sweating and dripping all inside of my shirt and down my back. She stopped for a minute and commanded me to turn off the heat because, "It is too hot in here."

Then she abruptly stopped counting the money and declared that all of the money was not there. She said that money was missing. Just hearing that made me almost want to pass out. I was hot in the worst way, from fear and the realization that I had not, no—WE— had not counted the money. So, she stopped and counted it again. She looked at me shook her head and said, "Nope. Not there."

By now, my shirt was soaking wet. I had taken off my jacket and loosened my tie and didn't know what the hell I was gonna do. I didn't want anyone to think I had stolen the money. The bookkeeper didn't accompany me to Ms. Franklin's dressing room. Not to mention, the bank wasn't going to believe or admit that we didn't get the right amount of money. The only thing that could possibly save me is the teller's drawer being long and not "short" which would show the error. Time stood still and I was frozen. My mind was the only thing moving. Racing!

I decided to ask her if I could count the money. I chose to put it in five thousand-dollar increments. I wanted her to see the stacks and she watched me very closely as I confirmed and had her approve each stack. I got to seventy-five thousand dollars and by that time, I needed a shower. She looked at the money and said okay.

Luckily, I lived right in the next town over, but it was really just like up the block and around the corner. I ran home, showered, and changed. What a blessing that I didn't have a different outcome because I believe she would have called off the show had her money not been right. I didn't see her waiting until the next day for me to rectify the situation. Aretha was a true diva! She ain't take no mess. R.E.S.P.E.C.T! She definitely showed people what it meant!

When the show began that night, in her true Aretha Franklin M.O., her bag full of money was on the piano. Now that I think about it, maybe Aretha was the inspiration for getting money being called, "getting to the bag!"

## CHAPTER 47

# LOOK AT ME NOW

I have so many stories to tell, they could fill a library of books. There was never a dull moment, so while most of my stories are unbelievable, they are also all true. Often when I met with an artist at the theater, I would greet them at the door, walk with them, get acquainted, and just be hospitable as I escorted them to their dressing room.

When I met Ms. Etta James, I was extremely excited, but I was also cool and laid back. I was used to celebrities. I was never star-struck. *(Well, maybe when I worked with Eddie Murphy…and Prince)*

At least I wasn't going to be acting all weird and freak anybody out. I knew how to conduct myself professionally, be cordial, and still have my natural swag.

When I met Ms. James, I spoke to her, but she did not respond. I found it odd that she didn't really give me any eye contact. But even more crazy was the fact that we got on the elevator, and she looked straight ahead and said, "Don't fucking look at me." I did not reply, looked straight ahead, and let her in the room.

When I returned to give her the check, she was sitting with the door open at her vanity mirror, putting on her makeup. I tapped on the open door. I dare not step in. She turned around and said, "Get away from my fucking door, and close it."

I replied, "I was coming to bring your check to you."

She said, "I don't care. Close my fucking door and slide the check under it."

I did as she requested. Let's just say it was an uneventful night. Often, the nights were memorable, but that was usually when the artist has good spirits. I was so excited to meet her and it was disheartening to have that be the experience.

One of the best shows I had at Bergen PAC was a show with Chris Brown, Ne-Yo, and Trey Songz. Chris had just come out with his record and his road manager, Andre Thorpe, told me to book him and that I wouldn't be disappointed. Wendy Credle, the attorney for Ne-Yo,

*Mark Green, Chris Brown, and Andre Thorpe*

requested that he be put in the show as well. I had already booked Trey Songz, who was blowing up the charts. Out of nowhere, the chairman of the theater came and asked me who were these people that I'd booked. I explained but he was not impressed. No sooner than I suggested he ask his daughter if she had heard of them, the show sold out. He asked for twelve tickets for his daughter, but the show had already sold out. He told me to figure it out. I put a row of folding chairs in front of the stage and in front of the first row of sold-out seats. He also wanted a "meet and greet" arranged. I adhered to all his requests and made it happen for him.

After the show, I was approached by a local magazine out of N.J. They wanted to give me my props for taking the theater and transforming it into a place for live music and performances and making it more than just cultural shows. Not only did they interview me, but they put me on the cover of the magazine. Well, that did not sit well with some of the employees. One thing it did was show me who was *for* me and who was *against* me. There were those who congratulated me and then there were those who said nothing. I even witnessed one guy throw the magazine on the floor. I didn't care because my face was in every store in Bergen County, and I was enjoying myself and my life. I was enjoying my shine. Parties, strip clubs, trips, dinners, and expensive clothes. I could basically buy whatever I wanted. Unfortunately, I couldn't repair my marriage, which was suffering, to say the least. I was always in the streets, more than I was home. Sheila, my employee, and I began to have problems and I was getting frustrated with her and knew I had to bring it to an end. After twelve years of employment, I had to let her go.

I was hanging out a little too much, leaving my wife behind. Then one day, it happened! My wife asked for a divorce and I was devastated. I could not understand what was going on. She had begun to hang with Sheila and they developed a long-lasting friendship. I, on the other hand, was headed into a deep depression. Carmen had her mind made up and there was no turning back. Everything came to a halt.

My life was about to change but just how drastically, I had no idea.

I needed to get to the bottom of who was involved, what was really going on, and when all of this started to take place. I remember riding around town searching for some answers with my gun in tow.

At work I stayed to myself, did not talk to anyone, and smoked a pack of cigarettes a day. I really needed help. Finally, I called my pastor. It was his conversation that brought me to realize that my wife was gone and not coming back and ultimately, I needed to make a change in my life. We had several conversations that helped me tremendously. It was his testimony that allowed me to seek some help and focus on his words.

Out of the blue, a guy who I had not really cared for became my mentor and life saver. His name was Peter and he was Sheila's boyfriend. He stayed with me and kept me at peace as if I was his son. I can't begin to thank him for his words of encouragement, his leadership, and making sure I stood tall during my downfall. I would call him day and night no matter what time it was and he would answer. He always delivered peace to bring me back from despair.

During that time, the theater was seeking a new director and I had no interest or desire to apply for the role. I enjoyed the position I had as general manager. It aligned better with my skills and expertise. Eventually, someone else was brought in. In the beginning, the director and I got along well. Then we started having differences of opinion. Not to mention, he noticed that I would disappear for fifteen, or sometimes, thirty minutes. One day he followed me and saw me in the alley on the phone. I saw him out of the corner of my eye. I knew I had to tell him what was going on because I looked suspicious. So, I did.

"Danny, I'm going through a divorce and I leave the office to sulk and pray."

He was glad I told him because he thought I was hiding out doing drugs or something.

## CHAPTER 48

# SHE'S NOT JUST ANOTHER WOMAN

My first year after the divorce, I began to come around a little bit but I was still not looking or feeling like myself. I had gained weight and I was going bald. As the holidays approached, I felt worse. Then I decided I needed to go on a date. But I had been married for so long, I didn't know how to date. I decided to sign up for online dating and I spent about $8,000 on a new wardrobe.

Online dating was new and the stories I have could be a separate book. I had no idea what to expect but after doing it for more than three years, I learned how to navigate through the madness. Some of the people I met along the way have become good friends, and others I see on Facebook and other social media platforms. I truly was not ready to date as several women would tell me later but it at least gave me something to do.

One of my first encounters was with a woman named Mary. She was Puerto Rican and lived in Brooklyn. She had a great job working in health care and had a young son who lived with her. Mary had the makings of being a great wife.

She had her own condo, a master's degree in her field, and she was very good looking. We are still friends today, although there was no love connection back then. What we found was true friendship. We both were going through similar situations so we leaned on each other for advice. We would discuss our dates and talk about what we did right or wrong. I thought I knew everything about women, but I was wrong. Weekly dating gave me more than enough to understand.

As men, we think it is all about love and conquering a woman, but it is more than that. I really began to understand what women wanted and what they truly like in a relationship. Every date was an interview for me and the more I interviewed them, the more I regained my confidence.

The funny thing is every woman I met on the dating sites lied about their age and weight (Lol). I would meet women who posted photos of themselves that were three to five years old. I once went out with a doctor and when I got to the restaurant to meet her, I couldn't find her. Suddenly, an old lady started flagging me down. After our introduction, I asked her why she posted a photo of herself when she was young. She said she hoped that after I met her, her personality would win me over. I laughed and said yes, but I want the girl in the photo. Needless to say, we became friends and that was the extent of it.

The first year of dating, I had no interest in being intimate with anyone. I was still depressed and withdrawn. That did not sit well with some of my dates. Some of those women acted like dogs in heat. They were ready to do whatever. I consider myself a person of good character, choices, and taste, but you can't judge a book by its cover and sometimes the story in the book is nothing but a fantasy or a set-up waiting to happen.

One night I went out with a woman who seemed like an around-the-way girl who was also smart. We were at dinner having a decent conversation until I told her I needed to use the restroom. As I got up to go, she said, "While you're in there, take a photo of your penis and send it to me." Unfortunately, I did not heed to her request, and as we continued on with our meal, it became obvious that she was more interested in what was in my pants than what was on her plate. As we were leaving the restaurant, she suggested that we go back to her place but I had no interest in her. I decided to go home, and we never spoke again.

I was so desperate to find love that I did not care about the woman's background. So, I went out with every nationality you can name. I dated Jewish, Italian, Jamaican, Korean, Indian, Japanese, Haitian, Columbian, Dominican, Puerto Rican, Irish, and of course Black.

I was also trying to regain my relationship with God, so that became a big part of my conversation while dating, and that did not sit well with some. I met four atheists, and I don't have to tell you that those dates ended quickly. There was no way I was going to be with anyone who was not God-fearing or doubting His greatness.

Then I met a girl from Philly. We went out about three times only to find out that she was a stalker. I can't even go into all that happened. However, in the end, I had to go to court to rid myself of this lady and while I was filing a report, found out she had multiple identifications and names. It was suggested to me not to divulge all of my business in court, knowing the nature of this woman. My dirty laundry needed to stay in the bag, which brings me to ***Rule #3: Keep your Mouth Shut.***

One day I decided to have a party at my house and I invited every girl I went out with and six of them showed up, including the doctor. My friends were happy because I brought sand to the beach for them to enjoy, but I still was not ready. Then there were the ones I liked but they had no interest in me. The first year of dating I was not myself. I had no idea who I was or what I wanted. I just needed to be happy again. One of the things that helped me was Steve Harvey's new book, *Think Like a Man and Act Like a Lady*. It really brought back the perspective of dating and how to choose a mate.

## CHAPTER 49

# GANGSTA LUV

I n the meantime, work at my job began to restore and things were back to normal. However, after three years, the relationship between me and the director soured. The chairman added to the problem by playing us against each other. So, eventually Danny decided to let me go under the guise of restructuring.

I saw it coming as he let a couple of other people go before me. When he called me into his office, I had already been

*Mark Green & Montel Jordon*

deleting my files. They weren't going to use me, let me go, and keep my contacts.

No sooner than I got fired, I got a call to book Montell Jordan for a show in Brazil. I decided to go with the crew on the trip since I was unemployed. Montell Jordan was rapper on Def Jam who had several hits but the one that people identify him with is "This is how we do It."

The flight was ten hours too long but Brazil was beautiful. When we arrived, we were greeted by a lady who was apparently the promoter. When she caught my eye, I was intrigued by the fact that she had four bodyguards. I wanted to know why she had such high security. Come to find out, she was the wife of a mafioso boss. She was trying to make a name for herself and have her own business. She treated us like royalty.

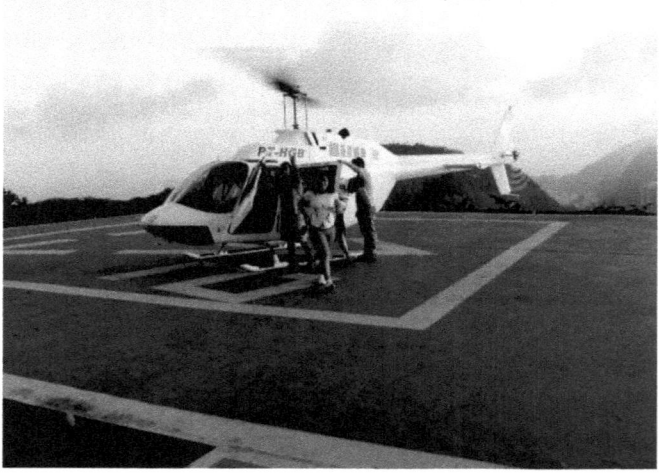

The first thing she did was take us to a restaurant that she had closed down just for us to dine without fanfare. The next morning, she offered us a sightseeing tour to see the city. I thought we were going to drive around. We had no idea she was going to take us up in the air. We climbed a big hill to a heliport and there was a helicopter waiting for us. I had never been on a helicopter and the sight of sitting next to the door that opened, sent shock waves to my brain. I was jetting around Brazil seeing the sights and although it was beautiful and I felt important, I also felt like I could fall out of the helicopter and die at any second. I already had a fear of heights and flying, so you can image how I felt in that cockpit.

I kept my cool and focused on the landmarks. The Christ the Redeemer statue looked like it was tall enough to reach up to heaven for real. I couldn't even figure out how they were able to build such a gigantic statue on top of a steep mountain peak. It is something you have to see to believe and one of the 7th wonders of the world. The other place was the famous Maracanã Soccer Stadium.

I wanted to go to a mall to shop and get some souvenirs to give out when I got back home. I was looking for a mall like back home. However, she took us to one of the most expensive malls there. Out of nowhere, she asked Montell if he wanted some jewelry for his wife and she bought a diamond cross necklace for Montell's wife. She treated us to whatever we wanted and bought everything. She bought me three Brazilian bathing suits for my imaginary girlfriend because I wasn't proud to admit that I didn't have one at the time when she asked, so I just accepted the gifts.

We went back to the hotel to get dressed for the show. We were picked up by three blacked out and bulletproof SUVs, that came with two bodyguards per car. We rode in the middle vehicle. When I got to the show, she asked if I wanted anything to drink. When I replied yes, she sent over a case of MOET. Needless to say, I could only drink one bottle so I gave the rest to the groupies that followed us.

After the show, she insisted that we go out on the town. The nightlife was live and when we arrived at the club, the bodyguards walked in front while a few stayed behind. The weirdest thing happened. The bodyguards checked in their big 9 mm Glocks at the coat check. The thought of checking your guns at a coat check still amazes me. I didn't know whether to feel nervous that they didn't have them on them or happy about the same.

The bodyguards didn't let us out of their sight, even to go to the bathroom. They were everywhere I turned. Thank God nothing transpired that night. It was just a night full of unlimited money, drinks, and worries. I was so glad nothing prompted the guards to have to show that they were prepared for war, not to mention they only spoke Portuguese. Brazil was beautiful and the experience for the three days was unbelievable.

## CHAPTER 50

# DO THE HUSTLE

When I returned to the States, I was in hustle mode and I knew I had to make some changes in my life, starting with shutting down my office. It no longer made sense. I had a big four-bedroom house I lived in alone but was paying for an office I did not go to. So, I moved everything home and set up shop there.

I applied for unemployment and during that time, Obama was allowing three years of unemployment. I did not want to waste any time, so I signed up for Venue Management School. I decided to take the down time and go back to school to get my certification in Venue Management.

One thing I've done every year for the last eighteen years is to learn a new trade, take an online course, get a new certification, or just learn something new. Over the years, I have received certificates and licenses in Bartending, CPR, Event Safety Training, Gun Safety, Fire Guard, Salsa lessons, Venue Management (Graduate program), Food and Beverages, Covid-19 Compliance, Spanish, Business Management, received a black belt in Taekwondo and a red belt in Karate, published a book, (The Grandmaster Flash Story), and many more. In addition, writing this book, my first book. I am glad I will have something to leave behind about the industry that made my dreams come true.

The break in time was just enough for me to regroup and reinvent myself. As I was getting myself together, I decided to rent a room out of my house for a steady income. I went on Craig's list at the advice of a friend. I was renting out my upstairs master bedroom. I also had other rooms that were vacant. I got a lot of interested responses, until they saw me in the flesh. Everyone from Asian, Indian, White, and Caribbean. None of them could wrap their heads around me being the homeowner. The thought of them having to pay me money to stay in my house was too far-fetched for them. I had two people who immediately asked for the owner of the house as soon as I opened the door and when I said I was the owner, there was an obvious change in their demeanor.

Finally, a young guy from Iowa was ready to move in. He sent me the deposit with no issues but I was a little skeptical. I wanted to be comfortable sleeping in my house without having to keep one eye open at all times. The guy explained that he had just gotten hired by the Mercedes-Benz dealership and that my money would be guaranteed, because they were paying for his room and board.

## CHAPTER 51

# LADIES NIGHT

He moved in and we hit it off. We had no issues at all. He lived with me for about a year and when he left, he referred me to another worker from his dealership. The new guy happened to be from Germany. The dealership had come and inspected my home because they had a lot of new hires that were not from the area. They preferred to put them up in my place because a hotel bill would have been astronomical. I liked the business arrangement that I had with Mercedes Benz because my money was always paid on time. At the same time, a friend was going through a divorce and he needed a place to stay. I went from having one tenant to two and the ability to pay off a lot of bills and get back on my feet.

I also went back to online dating because Mrs. Right was just not coming to ring my doorbell. However, I began to enjoy dating online as I started to understand the games and the tricks people often play. I already knew that the photo online may not necessarily look like the person you were about to meet. I also knew to add anywhere from two to five years more to the age they claimed to be. I was also ready to become intimate. I wished I could snap my fingers and the woman of my dreams would appear but I kept clicking and ending up back at square one when things didn't turn out the way I expected.

One woman appeared to have potential and we dated for a year, even though she was not a favorite of my family or some of my friends. She lived with her brother in the town next to mine. She made mention that she had an apartment in NYC but was renting it out. It was later revealed that she was in an "immigration marriage." I just couldn't date someone who was living with a husband, even if it was a shell marriage. Also, I couldn't believe she never told me until a year in. The hard lesson learned there was that some women are just as shifty and conniving (and not as forthcoming) as they claim about men.

I had done my dirt and was no longer interested in playing games, so being more God-like and living more righteously was my goal. I had always attended church, but I was under more conviction about the things I did. I could no longer excuse away my bad behavior, but I had to acknowledge it and be real with myself about it and work deliberately to correct it. It's hard because it seems like just when you are trying to be better, all hell breaks loose.

I was online one night and saw a profile that piqued my interest. Everything she said caught my attention, but she was from Philadelphia and I was not sure if I wanted to do long-distance dating. I hesitated at first but decided to give it a try.

She seemed to feel the same way when she saw my profile. We decided to meet somewhere in South Jersey for dinner. We met at a place that was amazing. The atmosphere was out of this world and the place was beautiful. The bill was another story. We had an eight-course meal that looked good but left me unfulfilled, and definitely not worth the cost. I was devastated when the bill came because I could not adjust my mind to our $400 check. It seemed out of this world not to mention, I would have to leave an appropriate tip. Before I could say anything, my date suggested we split the bill. Whew! I agreed. The night ended with a smack on the lips and an "I look forward to seeing you again."

About a week later, I invited her to my home. She mentioned that she and a couple of friends were thinking about coming to Harlem to shop so I invited them to spend the night and she agreed.

They arrived early Saturday morning and I took them to Harlem. I stayed in my car and walked around on my own while they went shopping. On our way back to my house, we decided to stay in for dinner and have a movie night. That sounded good because I did not want to try and feed three women plus myself. Before I could say anything, the women decided to cook and I felt even better about the plan. They also gave me a house gift for my hospitality.

As the night came to an end, I stopped double-checking the girl I was about to date and really started feeling one of her friends. I tried not to show any interest, but her friend was who I wanted. When it came time to sleep, I gave everyone their own room, including my date. At the time, I didn't have any tenants so I had four bedrooms and there were four of us. She was not feeling that at all. She wanted to share my bed, but after meeting one of her friends, I was no longer interested in her.

The next day was intense. She was angry and questioned why I did not sleep with her. I gave her some lame excuse about it not being a good idea with all of her friends in the house and told her that I only wanted to spend time with her. She sent her friends home early that morning and decided to accompany me to church. Things seemed odd and I came across indifferent, so she went home right after church. I did not know if I was going to hear from her again, and I really didn't want to. There was something weird about her, but I couldn't quite put my finger on what it was. However, in the following weeks, she started to reach back out to me.

I decided to look more into who she was and it did not take long for me to find someone who knew her. Then it all started unraveling. The woman was not only crazy but turned out to be another stalker I had to block and threaten. I also found out her father was a prominent politician in Philadelphia and I will just leave that right there.

# CHAPTER 52

## HOW DEEP IS YOUR LOVE

After the last situation, I decided to try the dating site, Match. All the other sites were connecting me to crazy and unfit characters. I liked Match because it had more quality profiles and everyone seemed to have more professional backgrounds. That's when I met a beautiful woman named Yoselin.

I reached out to her first and it took her about three days to respond but when she did, I knew she was "The One." From the very first time we spoke on the phone, she had such a calming spirit, it locked me in. I had been praying hard for God to send me someone that was going to be *for* me. When I heard her voice, I knew. On our first date, it was confirmed even more.

I met her by her house and we went and got pizza. The conversation was limited because she was nervous and didn't speak very good English. She was Dominican and had been in the States for five years. I was not as fluent in Spanish anymore, but I was willing to relearn for her. The feeling was genuine though. When the date ended, I made it clear that I was interested in her and wanted to see her again soon.

Our next date was at an Italian restaurant in Clifton, where she was residing at the time. We were both more relaxed and fortunately, the vibe was still a good one. We had a lot in common. She liked salsa dancing, and I loved it as well. I had always been into Spanish culture, so it was intriguing to meet the girl of my dreams. I had visited the Dominican Republic during my divorce and loved the people and their loving spirits. The women know how to cater to men, and

*Yoselin Green*

they seem very united as a people. Dominicans are family-oriented, so meeting Yoselin felt like home. She was everything I was looking for.

After dating for slightly more than four months, we were planning to bring our families together to meet. Yoselin had a son, Jose, who I had already met. He was about eight at the time. I had a birthday coming up, so Yoselin purchased some items from my daughter's online store for me in support of Janay before meeting her, which was nice. Unfortunately, they never actually met. When my father and cousin met her, they made sure to let me know that I should marry her. That was my confirmation that I had finally met my wife.

The following week, I decided to go back to college to get my master's degree. I was taking courses part-time and not in school for longer than a month when I received a devastating phone call during class one day.

My daughter's mother, Victoria, called and told me I needed to get to Virginia immediately. My daughter had been in a car crash and was in bad shape. I dropped everything and jumped on a plane to Virginia. When I got to the hospital and saw my daughter, I was floored to see her unconscious and with several tubes in her. I prayed and was hopeful that she would come out of it. I assumed everything would eventually be okay. It wasn't until the next day that they told me she was already brain-dead.

Janay was traveling during a rainstorm. She was driving alone and, unfortunately, began to hydroplane and collided with another vehicle. No one in the other car was badly hurt and although my daughter died, they still sued. I was devastated trying to deal with the death of my daughter when I received a call from the other party's lawyer regarding a lawsuit. I can't believe someone could be so insensitive. Not to be cliche, but when it rains, it pours. Every time it rains, I think of my baby girl and all the future moments we will never get to spend together. When things like this happen, you start thinking of all you should have done and asking for healing at the same time.

This type of loss is indescribable. There is no real way to express the pain or feeling of loss. No words exist to accurately explain how a parent feels after losing a child. You can only come close to understanding if you've had to endure it. It's like being a member of a club that you never imagined being in. You wish every day that you could turn back time and not have to know that depth of loss and pain. I don't wish it on my worst enemy.

On the third day in the hospital, everyone in my family was there for support, along with two of my frat brothers, Eric Johnson, Marshall Nelson and his wife, and my cousin Otis Harrison. They were just as devastated as me and Janay's mom. My sister Lori was there along with my parents, who were heartbroken to see their granddaughter in such a state.

*Mark Green & Chico Gibbs*

Another friend of mine, Chico Gibbs, heard about what happened and flew in from Dallas. I was shocked to see him. He came in and assisted with the handling of the funeral arrangements which took a huge load off our family.

By the fourth day, we were told that Janay would spend the rest of her days on life support. Her mother and I decided that that was no life for her to live and prepared for her to go on to be with our Lord.

We decided to have her organs donated. When she was removed from life support, they waited for her to "pass on." It was twenty minutes, but it felt like twenty hours. As soon as she was considered deceased, they rushed her body out to perform the surgeries. Time stood still but my heart was so full of grief that I didn't know what to do or how to really react. Just watching everyone counting the time and waiting was unbearable. I kept walking in and out of the operating room because I could not take it. I was sad and horrified.

I cried for days and nights on end. I was lost and hurt. One of my frat brothers, Tony McGriff, insisted I let him come stay with me during that time. I had refused at first but just having him present helped me see my way through. It is something you never get over but must learn to live with. Tony was a life savior.

The funeral was held a couple of days later. We decided to have a closed casket. Even though we hadn't been dating for long, Yoselin attended the funeral with me. It was not a great way to start a relationship, but I knew not many women would have been able to handle such a heavy situation in the beginning. She felt my pain and was there for me.

During my daughter's funeral, I was surprised at all the people who showed up—frat brothers, cousins, and friends, to support me through that heartbreaking time. They say you see who your friends really are when you go through something tragic. The love was so appreciated and comforting. Many of Janay's classmates were in attendance and her former high school decided to create a scholarship in her name. I am proud of the legacy she left. She will never be forgotten. I would have liked to meet the people to whom her organs were donated, but just knowing that her final act on earth enabled others to live, warms my heart.

*Mark Green & Janay Green (Daughter)*

CHAPTER 53

# WEDDING BELL BLUES

It took me a long time to feel normal again after Janay died. I walked around kind of out of it. I had ongoing support from friends who helped me continue the scholarship the second and third year, as the school only contributed funds the first year. When the dust settled, many friends and family members let me down when they wouldn't donate a mere $25 in honor of my daughter's scholarship. Like I said before, you see people's true colors when you are going through something bad, especially when money is involved. But my daughter was worth more than anything money could buy so I had to cut ties with some people because they showed me they were not concerned with keeping her legacy alive. Through it all, there was Yoselin. And she was there every step of the way.

When I returned back home, Mercedes Benz wanted to send me another tenant but I already had two tenants, Todd and Juan. Todd Franklin was a new friend I met through an old friend. He had attended the same college as me, but five years later. We had a great relationship and are still good friends. Things were calm, but I got tired of having a bachelor pad. I also got tired of the dirty dishes and paying for a cleaning service to keep us in order. One year later, I informed them that they needed to find another house to hang out in because I wanted to turn mine into a home.

One day, I woke up and decided I was going to purchase a ring and propose to Yoselin. I had been contemplating the move for a long time, trying to wait for the best moment. I wanted the moment to be special and I wanted family present. The perfect way to accomplish that was the day that my block association had its annual block party. It is always filled with fun, family, and love. The event took place every year around the last week in July and the first week in August, and it was a time when our families always came together.

That day, Yoselin's family came to enjoy the outside festivities. I approached her brother and informed him of my plans to ask his sister to marry me. I also asked him to translate my intentions to their father in Spanish. Her father gave his blessings through his son and it was a go! In the evening, we moved the party indoors. Before we were ready to say grace and eat dinner, I told everyone I had an announcement. I took a deep breath, got down on one knee, and took Yoselin's hand. When she saw me looking up at her with the box in my hand, she was elated and began to cry. She said yes!

I was happy but a bit concerned about my employment status. I knew I was ready to marry her, but I had to line everything up so the timing would be right. I was in the last months of the third year of unemployment.

Yoselin and I were in our second year of dating and now being engaged, we started to discuss the wedding. I was a little nervous—nope, I was a lot nervous because I still had no job, and I wanted a job before we got married. It was not long before my family asked what my intentions were and I expressed to my father that I was gun shy due to not having a job. That's when he hit me with the one-two punch. He said, "You have a very good girl. We all like her. So what, you don't have a job. You'll get one soon. What's the difference if you get married and you lose your job the next month? You would still be in the same position. If you let her go now, you can forget about her coming back."

I took what he said into consideration, but at that time, I was going to leave it to God. I prayed on it and he answered my prayer. We got married within the year. It was a beautiful wedding. But I'm a man and most men are raised to be providers. Yes, I was happy to be with the love of my life, woman of my dreams, and life partner. But I was in no financial position to have the wedding that my wife would have loved to have, although she was happy. We didn't have a big wedding and could not extend an invitation to a lot of friends or even cousins. It was strictly parents, aunts, and uncles and of course, no kids.

Let's just say a lot of people didn't talk to me for a long time because of the limited guest list. Some of my frat brothers and "boys" decided to crash the wedding. I just want to apologize for making anyone feel left out. The best thing is that twelve years later, we are still together, and "No man can put asunder what God had brought together."

## CHAPTER 54

# I'LL BE MISSING YOU

Two months after our wedding, I got a disturbing phone call from my sister Lori, telling me to come to my parent's house. When I got there, I found out that my mother had passed away that morning in her sleep. I had just lost my daughter and now my mother. I was devastated. It was shocking that my mother passed so early, considering she was the youngest of her siblings. She died at eighty-two, and all of her older siblings, except one, are still kicking into their late 90s. You just never know. That's why you must cherish every day.

Before I could fully process losing my mother, Yoselin was diagnosed with breast cancer a month later. My mother had just died in June, only a year after my daughter. Talk about raining and pouring. Then came the hurricane.

We received a medical bill for $20,000. Although I had insurance, I was under covered. I went through a whole ordeal of dropping my insurance, picking up coverage under the Affordable Care Act, which still wasn't enough, and then being advised by a friend, Joanne English, to apply for Charity

Care. Joanne is a prominent realtor out of Englewood and has a charity for supporting breast cancer survivors like herself. I had no idea what Charity Care was or how to apply for it, but we applied and that's when things got interesting.

They wanted all of my financials and they were sizing me up to decide if I was going to get the coverage. They wanted to know how I could drive a Mercedes and hold onto a house for three years without any income. Although it was a challenge because we needed certain documents to qualify, I did what I had to do and we received 100% coverage. We didn't have to pay anything! I must give the glory to God because He led me through the fire and I never doubted Him!

Yoselin has been in remission for ten years. Thank God!

## CHAPTER 55

# HE SAW THE BEST IN ME

I t was time to get back to the bag. I had been looking for another job for months that turned into years. During the third year of unemployment, I got offered a position to be the Supervisor of Food and Beverage at MetLife Stadium. It was different from most of my previous roles. My job was to oversee ten food stands and to troubleshoot any issues during the game and after. At the end of the night, I had to go to each stand and check the paperwork. If the paperwork did not match the money in the cash register, we had to go back and fix the problem.

My problem was that I had about six useless stand managers that always had problems and I could not leave until the problem was resolved. On any given day, I would start work at 7 a.m. and sometimes would not leave until 2 a.m. Eighteen hours for a BS job that was only paying $2.00 more than a stand manager. It definitely wasn't what I was used to and my ego was busted. It wasn't glitzy or glamorous. I couldn't fathom that my life in entertainment would end with me being in charge of plates and cups.

It was humbling but like anything else, you don't catch the lesson during the struggle. It is after you have proven to yourself that you can endure and get to the other side, that you learn that it (whatever it may be) is usually for character-building or an experience that you don't realize you need. I learned to appreciate what I was given, even if it wasn't what I asked for because life can always be worse. Someone else always has a situation that you would not choose. *(Rule #8: Don't Take Menial Jobs for Granted)*

This led me to think about God, my life, and all the things that He had brought me through. Especially the many times that my time could have run out. I thought about the drugs, the guns, the company I kept, and all the missed opportunities that could have ended with me buried six feet under. Like the song "Tears of a Clown," no one knew the pain I had inside. I decided to commit myself to God, to focus on His word, and to see what else He had in store for me. That same weekend, I attended church and rededicated my life to Christ.

"God may not come when you want Him, but He is always right on time." His time. And His timing and blessings are always better than ours. I could have made a complete mess of my life, as I had unknowingly tried to but He stepped in every time and saved me. I had to stand on His promises and know that things would get better.

Out of the blue, Grandmaster Flash came calling for the third time. He wanted me to manage him again and I did. I was doing okay with my income from MetLife Stadium, my tenants, and a few bookings here and there. Now with Flash in the mix, I was comfortable again.

I had been applying for job after job and kept getting

rejection after rejection. It was like my experience didn't matter. No one was hiring me. But I could still see God working in my life though. I stayed in prayer, and stayed faithful to His Word and on His promises because I know He will be with me at all times.

I was overlooking all the resumes I'd submitted and came across one I had sent to Madison Square Garden. I reached back out to them to see what happened with my application. When I called HR around 11 a.m., they told me they had overlooked my resume but asked if I could come in at 2 p.m. because it was the last day of interviews.

Of course, I made it there in time. I was the last person to be interviewed for the job and I made a good impression even though I wasn't qualified based on the job description. The position was an Operational Supervisor and meant for a retired police officer. I had no experience as an officer, but I knew how to run a theater. I was hired! The job included sixteen supervisors who collectively dealt with the ins and outs of running a large concert venue/sports arena. I learned a lot about running a tight ship. I honed in and developed strong leadership skills because their rules and procedures were strict and demanding.

One thing is for sure and three things are for certain, I didn't get that job on my own merit or effort. Let me run this back for you in case you missed it. I'd put in an application months earlier and never received a call. I called on the LAST DAY of interviews. I was the last person to be interviewed and got the job, although I was underqualified. It is my job and my duty to give the glory where it should be. God qualified me. That one thing is for sure. He gave that to me. The two other things that are for certain is that the Father, Son, and Holy Spirit have guided me my whole life, from the hospital bed to Madison Square Garden.

While I was at the Garden, I started receiving calls from my former director at Bergen PAC. She was interested in having me come and work with her at Lehman College as the general manager for their theater. I had already turned her down twice because I was doing well working at the Garden, MetLife Stadium, managing Flash, and operating my talent agency, Celebrity Talent Agency. Things were going well.

The last time she called, I noticed things started to break down at the Garden when they hired a new general manager and he began to replace all the top senior executives. Sometimes, there is a warning sign that things are about to go awry. You have to get ahead of the storm, when possible.

I called the director back and she set up the interview. The four-panel interview included board members, a provost, and a college professor. After several days, they called me back to offer me the job. I accepted but continued to work at the Garden. Only because they said I would have to wait one month to get my first check. Although I stayed at Madison Square Garden for a while, as soon as I decided to go and work full-time at Lehman, they fired all the supervisors. Look at God. Wow, what timing! **God was directing my path.**

I was working at five jobs at one time, because I was scared to let any of them go. If you've ever been unemployed, you already know. I was in heavy rotation!

## CHAPTER 56

# HOLLYWOOD SWINGING

I was in my office when I received an email asking if I represented Flash. I responded yes and later got a phone call from a movie producer named Baz Luhrmann. Baz was the director of "The Great Gatsby," "Romeo and Juliet," "Moulin Rouge," and "Elvis." When he first called, I was surprised that he was reaching out to me. We spoke and he told me he wanted to have Flash in the movie that he was directing about the Disco Era and New York City. During my time managing Flash, I would get these types of calls all the time so when Baz called, I thought it was some BS until I searched him and saw exactly who he was.

We met several times in the city and he had everything outlined on how he wanted the movie to go. It lacked clarity on whether Flash was the main focus and character, but it turned out that it was more about the era than Flash. It wasn't just about him. The show, "The Get Down," ran eleven episodes with a character playing Flash.

Although I negotiated the deal, I felt kind of slighted after I began to investigate the whole movie deal. I leveraged more money for Flash to appear at promotional events. This allowed me to recoup some more money that I felt Flash should have received for his deal. We traveled all over, from the U.S. to the U.K. and back. Flash was doing demonstrations and press events and each time, I made them pay us $10,000 dollars for each appearance and demo. When it was all said and done, we made an additional $100,000 plus. The show took Flash to another level of fame and notoriety because younger people knew who he was. As he got bigger, so did the voices in his ear.

Everyone began to claim that they could do this and that for him. His star was continuing to climb higher into the heavens and unfortunately, I was left behind and replaced by his

*Mark Green, Grandmaster Flash, and Baz Luhrmann*

attorney as his new manager. This was my third time being fired by Flash, but I knew the deal when I accepted the gig. It was no big thing, because I had managed many artists in the past and there is no loyalty or longevity in artist management.

One good thing I am proud of regarding Grandmaster Flash is that I am responsible for getting his name trademarked. When I found out his name was not trademarked, I immediately got my lawyer to make it a priority.

## CHAPTER 57

# DANCE TO THE DRUMMER'S BEAT

Although I was able to protect Flash and his name, I was unable to protect myself and Master Gee (Sugarhill Gang) from Sugar Hill Records. First, I give all honor and respect to the late Sylvia Robinson, and her husband, Joey Robinson. I already mentioned that I started under their wing in the beginning of my career and would never have anything disrespectful to say about either one of them.

I cannot wholeheartedly say the same for Joey Robinson, Jr. We never had any problems while growing up together. We were introduced in the late 70s. However, Joey took on a new personality as he got older and was much different from the guy I knew.

I will take a moment to tell the truth and nothing but the truth, especially to quell all the confusion and rumors that swirled around our small towns regarding business that I had with the Sugarhill Gang and how it ended.

The Sugarhill Gang was the first rap group to be played on the radio in 1979. You can go to any wedding across cultures, religions, and ethnic groups and hear "Rapper's

Delight" played during the reception. The Sugarhill Gang was formed by Sylvia Robinson and made up of two rappers from Jersey and one from the Bronx. Their first song was a hit selling more than 14 million copies as of 2011 and etching itself into Hip-Hop history.

Master Gee, Wonder Mike, and Big Bank Hank said:

*"Now what you hear is not a test: I'm rappin' to the beat*
*And me, the groove, and my friends are gonna try to move*
*your feet.…"*

And we can't forget the part that everyone loves to say:

*"But first I gotta bang bang the boogie to the boogie*
*Say up jump the boogie to the bang bang boogie*
*Let's rock, you don't stop*
*Rock the riddle that will make your body rock!"*

The first time I heard rap during that DJ battle in the Bronx, I was hooked. I think Rakim sums up my first experience in his song "Move the Crowd." It was something new and cool and we just did it for fun. Who knew that fifty years later, this would be the number-one genre of music? I want to thank Master Gee for giving me props for introducing him to this new art form of music.

In 1984, Master Gee left The Sugarhill Gang and Sugar Hill Records. He came back in 2005 and I had already been booking Joey on shows as the Sugarhill Gang. The other group members had continued to work under and tour with Joey Jr. But in 2005, Master Gee and Wonder Mike began touring together as well.

Master Gee called me to book them and I mentioned to him that Joey had been going out on tour as Master Gee while he himself was not. I told him that he couldn't use the name because Joey and his "crew" had been using it for more than a decade. When Hank and Wonder Mike were not touring, other people were basically pretending to be them. They were getting booked for ten years.

Master Gee was aware that they had been going out as the Sugarhill Gang but he consulted with his lawyer who advised him that he and Wonder Mike could go out as "Master Gee and Wonder Mike, formerly of The Sugarhill Gang." After receiving the paperwork from Gee's lawyer, I started booking them for shows. When Joey found out that I was booking them, he came to me and demanded that I stop booking Master Gee and Wonder Mike. He told me he owned the name Master Gee. That's where it all went wrong. Joey had been keeping track of where they were being booked. He knew of every show they had. He told me to stop booking the group. I agreed but did not actually stop booking them. That is until someone showed up at my job with a subpoena for me to go to court.

I contacted my attorney who searched up the name and although the name "Master Gee" was free, and unclaimed, Joey had already submitted the petition for the name. He already owned the name, The Sugarhill Gang.

Joey filed a lawsuit against me for a quarter million dollars. It was crazy because although we weren't close friends, we had done business together and basically grew up together. A lot of people came to my defense and tried to talk some sense into Joey. I had artists, friends, and some of Joey's friends as well. But nothing could stop him. He felt like he had to teach me a lesson for not following his demands. I have been doing this for years. How did he think he was going to just shut my business down when he was basically not in the right either?

Joey asked me to show him the contracts I had of bookings dating back to 1999. Of course I didn't show him all the bookings, but what I showed him had $100,000 attached to it, and he wanted a piece of it. He said we could settle out of court for a hundred thousand but I kept asking myself, "What did I do wrong again?" and I kept getting the same answer in my head of "nothing."

It would have made more sense for the two of them to all come together and eat but Joey wasn't having it. I couldn't understand how he felt that he was entitled to another person's name who had had his name, way before the fame. It didn't make sense to me. Joey was used to getting what he wanted out of people and people being his peons. That, I could never be. But again, there was a lesson to learn. *(Rule #7: Never Underestimate the Other Person's Greed)*

## CHAPTER 58

# DEF BY TEMPTATION

The crazy thing about the whole situation was that I gave Joey his last show before he died. We finally came to a financial agreement and part of the deal was that I had to continue to book Joey's group. Somewhere in court, he was granted the name Master Gee, and now he was legit. I still don't understand how he was able to gain the name Master Gee but I guess there had to be some type of agreement. He was eager for me to book him, so he agreed to give me twenty percent versus the ten percent that I normally get. This was his way of saying, "Sorry, but I had to do it."

I was reluctant at the time and refused to even mention the Sugarhill Gang's name to any promoters. However, one day a promoter called and asked how much was the Sugarhill Gang. At the time, they were only getting $3,500 per show. So unwillingly, I said $10,000 and the promoter ok'd the deal. Before I could get happy, he came back with four more shows, all for the same price. I asked him what was going on and he said he books bar mitzvahs. Right then I made $10,000, not a bad start to recoup my money.

The last show Joey booked was a regular show and after the show, the promoter called to ask if Joey was okay. I asked why? He said that Joey had a hard time breathing and had to sit down during most of the show. He said he did not look well at all. When he asked Joey what was going on, Joey said he was recovering from the flu. The following day or so, Joey was rushed to the hospital with only weeks left to live. I wanted to see him before he passed but I wasn't granted permission. The sad thing is, I was at his father's, mother's, and his brother's funerals, and now I was at his. As I looked at him in the casket with the jewelry around his neck and diamond watch on his arm, I could only think about our journey together in this business and realize that nothing is promised for tomorrow. All the riches and the fame will soon dissipate…just like our lives one day.

Joey is no longer with us and at the end of the day, none of us can take our riches with us. Even if we had our prized possessions placed in the casket with us, they'd still remain as we transcend. I would hope that this also shows that we must not put money or material things above being fair and doing to others as we would have them do us. There are more important things than money. Things like justice, equality, integrity, character, and just being an up-standing person. Your legacy will follow you long after you die.

## CHAPTER 59

# HIP-HOP HOORAY

By now, Hip-Hop had begun to take over the music industry. Every radio station was playing it. Soul and Funk music were done. Only WBLS was playing classic R&B songs and a little bit of the new. Hip-Hop had now crossed over to white audiences, and millennials were eating it up. Rappers were dropping records in record speed and before you could learn the name of one artist, along came a new one.

Record companies started to realize how much money was in rap music. Not only was that change happening, but they were phasing out vinyl, and CDs were becoming the new format to listen to music. Record companies knew CDs would take over, so they began to offer the rap artist a higher royalty rate on vinyl and a lower royalty rate on CDs. Everyone was gung-ho, thinking they were getting over. In essence, they were being robbed.

Rap record deals were around $40,000 and the return on the money for the labels was almost twenty to thirty times that amount. Allegedly, M.C. Hammer convinced Capitol Records to invest in him and advance him a SIGNIFICANT amount of money on his first undisclosed record deal and it paid off when Capitol made over $30 million during his tenure with them.

On the other hand, Vanilla Ice was offered $30,000 by Def Jam but passed to take a deal with SBK (a part of Capitol & EMI Records) for $1.5 million. By now, every record label was trying to sign rap artists. This was the year that Capitol Records made so much money they gave all executives a 25% bonus on their salaries. By the early 90s, Hammer was ruling the charts. He had crossed over to mainstream and every white person who did not know how to dance was doing the Hammer dance moves. Rap was decidedly here to stay.

It would not be long before a new type of rap music would emerge. It was called Gangsta Rap. This new form of music started on the West Coast and began to catch fire on the East. Rap went from fun and ego stories to profanity and stories of killing and gang bangin. It was not too long before EMI got down with some West Coast groups by signing Compton's Most Wanted and Arabian Prince. For all the wrong reasons, the East Coast was still not willing to accept West Coast artists and songs. They were reluctant to play most of the music on the radio until it became impossible not to. Unfortunately, EMI had some of the worst rap records and for me, head of the rap department, I had to go to the stations and beg them to play my songs. I spent many nights with Chuck Chillout and Funkmaster Flex on WBLS sitting at the station waiting for my record to be played. I can hear Chuck's voice in my head. "Yo son, this shit is nervous." Or he would take my record and fly it across the room like a frisbee. "Yo son, this shit is wack."

By the end of the 90s and moving into the new millennium, you had more white people running rap labels than Black people. Then the rap artists began to set new rules on how business was done. Away went the real managers for rap artists. They were replaced by family members, friends, and later, thugs and gangsters.

By the mid-2000s, rap artists made booking agents change their business model as well. They demanded their money up front once the deal was done and deposits were made. No more waiting until after you played. You had to pay them before they committed to the date. That put a burden on agents because we became responsible for the artist's actions and for their appearance at shows. Promoters were not willing to release their money to an artist before they came to perform, but the demand for the artists were so great that they had no choice. It made agents completely responsible.

I got tired of trying to get the promoter and the artist to sign an addendum to the contract to release the funds. No one wanted to agree to the terms. I decided to put in my contract a clause that said by signing the contract, you give me permission to release the funds to the artist, manager, or their representative, with no further obligation to me, and that in the event the artist does not show up, it is the promoter's responsibility to get his/her money back from the artist.

That worked great for me because most promoters did not

read the fine print and just signed the contract. I'm proud to say that after being in this business for twenty-five years, I only got beat once for $3,000. Trust me, I spent about six months trying to get that money, including flying to the state looking for the dude and hiring someone to get the money for me.

It wasn't until I spoke to several promoters who told me my loss was nothing. They'd gotten beat for thousands of dollars. Regardless, I didn't care. I was still looking for dude with the gun in my pocket. But it took a promoter hitting me over the head with some common sense one day. He told me, "Stop it. If you mess around by sending someone after this guy and they accidentally kill him, your life is over. Or what if you mess around and catch him while you holding and shoot dude? You will be in jail for twenty to life. Is it really worth it for $3,000?"

I took his advice and kept it moving!

## CHAPTER 60

# THE LAST DANCE

It would be ten years later when I ran into another compromising situation with an artist named Ceelo Green. The year was 2010 and Ceelo came out with his hit song, *Fuck You*. It was not until February that the song started to catch fire outside of the U.S.

During that time, I scored him the opportunity to headline the biggest festival in Brazil. Things were initially great but as we got closer to the event, everything started to take a turn. Uncharacteristically, Ceelo (or his manager) demanded more money for the event. After the contract was signed, he wanted an additional $50,000 because his song had move up the charts, headed to the number one position. This was unheard of. How can you make this type of demand after the contract had been signed? The Brazil promoter was furious, but he needed Ceelo because he was the headliner. After days of going back and forth, they agreed to Ceelo's terms. They found out it was his birthday weekend and decided to go a bit further. They set up a big party with women, food, and drinks. They asked him to come in two days early to celebrate his birthday and show him real love.

He agreed and things seemed to be moving forward until the day came and he did not arrive in Brazil as planned. I immediately called his manager to see what was going on and his manager said Ceelo decided he wanted to go to Miami for his birthday instead. I could not believe what I was hearing. Not to mention, he already had half of the money! I went the fuck off and began losing my mind. But there was nothing I could do. They were not going to Brazil. In the meantime, before I could call the Brazilian gangsters to let them know, they were already in New York looking for me, Ceelo, and their money. They ran up to my satellite office only to find a P.O. Box Office and threaten the people there for my info.

By the next day, their attorney had arrived. I was already on the move. He tried to file a lawsuit, but my paperwork was on point. I starred in these "movie" scenarios many times and learned how to be the director of the movie and not the actor. They were not going to put me in a situation that I was unable to handle, so I got my own protection. I got in touch with Ceelo's manager and told him the gangstas were in the States demanding their money and looking for Ceelo. He immediately wired me the money. Without hesitation, I sent the money to the promoter and texted them to let them know that Ceelo was going to be a no-show. Unfortunately for me, they never responded and never did business with me again.

As time moved on, Hip-Hop went through more changes starting with the artist Drake. I remember when he first came out, he was asking for $200,000, and I said to myself, "Nobody is going to pay him that kind of money!" Little did

I know, he started getting that money all day. Within one weekend, he became a millionaire. Next thing I knew, all artists' fees started to hit the six-figure mark. Now we have artists like Cardi B getting upwards of $500,000 a show. It's a long way from the $1,500 artist used to get.

In case you don't know, Hip-Hop is here to stay and is another form of music that has created not just an avenue for money. but has become a culture that has transcended the world.

## CHAPTER 61

# BORN AGAIN

As agents, we deal with so many different issues as we present our artists to our buyers. There's never a moment to breathe or relax and feel that everything is okay. You are always one phone call away from a disappointment or a triumph, and it's never in order or etched in stone. You are always on go and on edge!

Many people see my career and the glitz of it, but believe me, there is no time to relax. You are just a phone call away from a lawsuit. There is no integrity, loyalty, or guarantee that the show will happen without any mishaps. We must always have a backup plan and stay one step ahead of the artist because even if it's not with that artist in particular, one thing for sure is that you better have your paperwork in order. Being a paper gangster is necessary, and the only way that you'll survive in this business. *(Rule #4 - Paper Gangsters Succeed)*

Just when you think everything is going great and you are at the beach relaxing, here comes a tsunami! And there is never a time to turn back because no matter what, *the show must go on!*

For all I have been through again, all praises to God!

\* \* \*

AT THIS MOMENT I am celebrating twenty-five years of owning my business and ten years as the Associate Director and General Manager of the Lehman Center for the Performing Arts. I'm also currently the Chair of Artist Relations for The Hip-Hop Museum. My roster of clients has now extended into the movie world, where I have worked with some all-time classic artists: Billy Dee Williams, Pam Grier, Larenz Tate, Derek Luke, Lou Gossett, Vivica A. Fox, Taye Diggs, Anthony Anderson, Boris Kodjoe, Shemar Moore, Spike Lee, Blair Underwood, Glynn Turman, Idris Elba, Lisa Raye, Morris Chestnut, Kimberly Elise, Lynn Whitfield, Richard Roundtree, Wendy Williams, Film Director Baz Luhrmann, and more.

As I look over my life, I can only give praises to God for protecting me and guiding me through the known and unknown. Although there were some hard lessons learned, the guidance and deliverance would not have happened if I had not been faithful to His Word. I have been in many compromising situations that could have ended my life on many occasions, but His grace and mercy shielded me.

It wasn't until I gave my life to Christ that I turned away from the bad decisions and the street lifestyle I was living. As people read my story, some may find it hard to believe because their impression of me is limited to being a nice guy. But know that everyone has a story and we've not all been privy to what everyone else has been through. We all have that "other side."

There are many people mentioned in this book that are no longer with us. I choose to tell my story to leave as a part of my legacy in this business and to remind all of us that we need to:

*Trust in the Lord with all thine heart; And lean not unto thine own understanding. In all thy ways acknowledge Him, and He shall direct thy paths.*

—Proverbs 3:5-6 KJV

# MY STREET RULES TO THE GAME

#1 **Trust No One**: Everyone has a motive.

#2 **Don't Believe the Hype:** Everyone has the best song, best artist, best production, the best game.

#3 **Keep Your Mouth Shut**: Those that tell don't know, and those that know don't tell.

#4 **Paper Gangsters Succeed**: Read everything more than once and keep an attorney on speed dial.

#5 **C.R.E.A.M: Cash Rules Everything Around Me** - Everything can be bought, including loyalty.

#6 **It Ain't Where You From, It's Where You're At**: "I don't care if you from New York, you in Ohio now." That's what he said when he had the gun to my head."

#7 **Never Underestimate the Other Person's Greed**: In negotiations, get what you can, while you can. People will try to take everything you have if you let them.

**#8 Don't Take Menial Jobs for Granted**: Learn what you can because the smallest thing will help you when you least expect it.

**#9 Keep Family and Friends Separate from Your Business:** I thought having family and friends around to watch my back was the best idea until I realized they were the ones stabbing me.

**#10 Trust Your Gut and Not Your Feelings**: Don't allow your emotions to dictate your moves.

# SPECIAL ACKNOWLEDGMENTS

First and foremost, I honor God for all His life lessons and blessings. I thank my Lord and Savior, Jesus Christ, for allowing me to walk again and saving me from the known and unknown circumstances. Through his saving grace, I am here to tell my story. For the Lord is my light and my salvation, of whom shall I fear? My faith in Him has been the guiding light in my journey.

Thank you to my mother, father, and daughter for supporting and believing in me. Although you are no longer here, your words and spirit live on.

Many people have played a significant role in my music industry journey, and I thank them for their love, support, and wisdom. For those who are no longer with us, your presence is deeply missed. I hope God is with you and we will reunite one day.

*My wife* – Yoselin Green, you were God sent. As we confess, it was nothing but God because our life started from the bottom, and within the first three months of our marriage, we encountered death, cancer, a language barrier, and joblessness. But through it all, you were there. I love you!

*My sister Lori* – Although we had our differences throughout childhood, we came together in the end. It was most needed, and I thank you for your love and trust.

***Author Ericka Williams*** – I have been a fan of your work for many years, and I want to thank you for coaching, teaching, and assisting me in this memoir. You breathed the words out of my mouth, making our partnership very comfortable.

***Dr. Jennifer L. Stoever*** – I can't thank you enough. You read my story, and without hesitation, you gave me direction and brought it to life. I am forever grateful.

***Chico Gibbs*** – You were there during the good and the bad. No matter what circumstance, my road dog, you stood by me.

***Penny Chan*** – My sister, thank you for your support, love, and friendship.

***Freddie Williams*** – we started in this entertainment business in eighth grade. You and your uncle have inspired me, and I am forever grateful.

***Louise West ESQ*** – You groomed, schooled, and taught me the real legal side of the business. I thank you with all my heart.

***Melba Moore*** – I can't thank you enough. You saw my passion, brought me in, and gave me my first job.

***Larry "Cognac" Johnson*** – We met on the Eddie Murphy tour 39 years ago and have done much together. Our friendship has stood the test of time, and our bond is unbroken.

***Jack Rannells ESQ*** – You represented me for over two decades and saved me from many legal situations. Thank you!

*Glynice Coleman* – You saw my potential and took me under your wing. You provided many years of employment, and I am forever grateful.

*Federoff Cohen* – Thank you for your friendship, words of encouragement, and all your help during the Eddie Murphy tour.

*Sheila Wade* – Thank you for your years of employment. We were together for twelve years. You stood by me through the good and the bad, and I thank you for your love, loyalty, and support.

*Dedra Tate* – Thank you for your love, friendship, and guidance. You have always been there for me and treated me like family. Thank you for introducing me to Renita Bryant and her company, Mynd Matters, who guided me through this process and made it happen.

*Renita Bryant and the team at Mynd Matters Publishing* – Thank you! Your professionalism, business, and company have been outstanding.

*There are so many people who have played a part in my career, and I want to thank you all:*

Londell Mc Millian, Mark Cheatam, Chuck Chillout, Kim Stuart, Shelia Wade, Varnell Johnson, Doug Daniels, Harry Coombs, Bobby Ducket, Kevin Harewood, Charles Huggins, Slyvia Robinson, Joey Robinson Sr., Jay Quan, Master Gee,

Tony Mc Griff, Barry Wells, Darryl "Krush" Kelson, Chuck D, Kurtis Blow, Angie Stone, Hilda Williams, Jodie Williams, Kimberley Thorton, Kim Thomas, Lillo Thomas, Tracey Jordon, Faith Newman, Reene Foster, Alica Underwood, Rocky Bucano, Funkmaster Flex, Todd Hardy, Saul &Nancy Brevard, Angela Thomas, David Rodriguez, Benny Pugh, Dedra Tate, Lynne Poole, Bo Samson, Rob Base, Chubb Rock, Rome JD, Rudy Shariff, Eddie LeVert Sr., Walter Williams, Toby Ludwig, Bobbie Douglas, Audrey Wheeler, Melisa Morgan, Alex Bugnon, Jackie Rinehart, Ed "Woodstock" Graves, Kool DJ Red Alert, Kevin Presley, Eric Sutton, Melle Mel, Karen Burton, Cherl da Pearl, Gino Shelton, Amp Harris, Grandmaster Flash, Guru, Sharon Heywood, James Boyce, Artie Reynolds, Jeanie Tate, Chubb Rock, Kool Moe Dee, Fred Buggs, Keith Ingram, Kevin Peck, Paul Tarnopol, Dru Hill, Usher, Al Goodman, Billy Jones, Joyce Harding, Harry Fobbs, Big Daddy Kane, Saquan Johnson, Johnny Washington, Sulliman Mausi, Lynette J. Blackwell, Betty Andrews, Yvonne Bach, Ki'a Stone , La Ron Tate, Rob Mason, Stuart Gray, Teena Marie, Frank Huttle, Todd Franklin, James Young, Geroge Harell, Jimmy Luv Jenkins, Andre Harell, Poggie Bell, Cindy Mizell, Shaila Scott, Herby luv Bugg, Donna Torence, Donna Davis, Oscar Cohen, Chris Webber, Stacey Murry, Tamara Eubanks, Leesa Waters, Adeola Busuyi, Kevin Baird, Natasha Anderson, Peter Harvey, Omega Psi Phi Spring 81 Nu Psi Chapter, Andre Thorpe, Venietia DiMarzo, Toni Willis, JT Taylor, Shakim, Freddie Jackson, Freddie Perren, Vicent Davis, Gene Rumsey, Henry Hen Dog, Victoria Spence,

Rodney Gillison, Fly Ty Williams, Will Smith, Jazzy Jeff, Phyllis Hyman, Larry Ward, Steve Branch, Mike Cameron/Al B Sure, Vincent Henry, Mike Austin, Mark Siegel, Paul Lamonica, Jerome Derrickson, David Heard, AJ Savage, Alina Kim, Virgil Thompson, Bob Celestin, Legendary Tony Sanders, Beau Huggins, Lance Hayes, & Chris Gardenhire.

www.ingramcontent.com/pod-product-compliance
Lightning Source LLC
Chambersburg PA
CBHW051608120626
46551CB00014B/1714